GUITAR LEGENDARY LICKS

GUNS N' ROSES

BY TOBY WINE

Recording credits: Doug Boduch, guitar • Warren Wiegratz, keyboard
Mark Solveson, bass • Scott Schroedl, drums
Recorded at Beathouse Music, Milwaukee, WI

Front cover photo by Ross Halfin

ISBN 1-57560-471-8

Visit our website at www.cherrylaneprint.com

About the Author

A freelance guitarist, composer, arranger, and teacher, Toby Wine lives in New York City and is a graduate of the Manhattan School of Music. Toby has performed with Philip Harper, Bob Mover, Joe Shepley, Ari Ambrose, Michael and Carolyn Leonhart, and John Ryerson, among others. His arrangements can be heard on Philip Harper's Muse CDs *Soulful Sin* and *The Thirteenth Moon,* and his composition "Venus" can be heard on soon-to-be-released CDs by Ari Ambrose (Steeplechase Records) and Ian Hendrickson Smith (Kpasta Records). Toby occasionally leads his own trio and septet, does studio recordings, and has worked as an orchestrator and score preparer for avant-garde innovator Ornette Coleman. In addition to work as an arranger and musical director for a variety of vocalists, Toby is also the music librarian for the Carnegie Hall Jazz Band and is a freelance writer (including the Cherry Lane publications *Steely Dan: Legendary Licks, The Art of Texas Blues,* and *Metallica: Easy Guitar with Lessons*) and editor. His studies have included work with Walter Davis, Jr., Bob Mover, Ken Wessel, Bern Nix, Ed Green, and Manny Albam.

Acknowledgments

Many thanks to the following folks for their help, influence, patience, and attention: Ari, Arthur, Bibi and Bob, Dave and Amy, Edward, Elizabeth, Enid, Gebb, Grits, Hong, Humph, Indiana Dave, Jack and Jack, Joe C, Kenny, Manny, Mark, Mover, Plum, Rebecca, Sammy, Smitty, and Thaddeus.

And especially my parents, Rosemary and Jerry.

Table of Contents

The Guns N' Roses Story 4
Guns Gear—Inside the Sounds 6
A Glimpse into Slash's Solo Style 8

From *Appetite for Destruction*
Welcome to the Jungle 11
It's So Easy 19
Mr. Brownstone 24
Paradise City 29
My Michelle 39
Sweet Child o' Mine 43

From *G N' R Lies*
Patience 51

From *Use Your Illusion I*
Live and Let Die 56
Don't Cry (Original) 59
November Rain 64

From *Use Your Illusion II*
Knockin' on Heaven's Door 68
Pretty Tied Up (The Perils of Rock N' Roll Decadence) 72

Guitar Notation Legend 77

The Guns N' Roses Story

Once in a while, a band comes along at precisely the right moment, filling a gaping void and setting the music world on its collective ear. Guns N' Roses was just such a band, and if you were one of the millions of people listening to "Welcome to the Jungle" in 1988, you may have felt as though they had materialized out of thin air, bursting onto the scene fully grown and relentlessly in your face. But, as is so often the case with bona fide sensations, the real story of their success is long, complicated, and fraught with struggles. On the other hand, like any good success story, the Guns N' Roses saga is also about the persistence, hard work, and belief in what they were creating that helped them fight through the hard times and reach the pinnacle of the rock 'n' roll mountain.

Our story begins with a "seeking a bass player" ad posted in L.A.'s. *Music Connection* newspaper by one Slash, a.k.a. Saul Hudson—an English-born, California-bred guitarist and son of the graphic artist responsible for countless Geffen album covers. Slash, raised in a show biz environment and unintimidated by L.A.'s wheelers and dealers, led bands playing original music throughout his high school days. His ad was answered by Michael "Duff" McKagan, a former drummer-turned-bassist and native of Seattle, Washington, who had literally just arrived in Los Angeles. Duff met with Slash and drummer Steven Adler, hit it off in a big way, and immediately joined their band, Road Crew (later, Hollywood Rose). This band was short-lived, but the boys had a fateful meeting with two transplanted musicians who'd moved west together from Lafayette, Indiana—vocalist W. Axl Rose (born William Bruce Bailey) and guitarist Izzy Stradlin (a.k.a. Jeff Isbell). The five men formed a new group with a two-guitar frontline. After several changes to the group's make-up, Axl and childhood buddy Stradlin both joined the popular club band L.A. Guns. A small tour up the coast was planned, but when their drummer (Rob Gardner) and guitarist (Tracii Guns) bailed out, Slash and Steven Adler got the call. The fivesome rehearsed for one week, played a gig at L.A.'s Troubadour nightclub, and hit the road for a disastrous but inspiring road trip. Broken down in the desert halfway to Seattle, the boys were forced to leave a U-haul full of equipment behind and hitchhike with their guitars the rest of the way. After playing for no money (and about ten people) in a deserted Seattle club, the band hit a low point—but they had no where else to go but up.

United by dedication and force of will, the five now felt closer, strengthened by the experience, and more determined than ever to get themselves into better venues. Returning to Los Angeles and shacking up together in a tiny room where they all ate, slept, and rehearsed, Guns N' Roses worked tirelessly, developing material and an unmistakable club-scene presence.

It was soon apparent that Guns N' Roses was doing something special and unique. They didn't fit into the neat boxes record executives loved and other L.A. bands were so eager to fill. True, they did possess more than a little bit of the fashionable, theatrical glam sensibility so pervasive at the time, but they were also meaner, rawer, and more influenced by both punk and classic Rolling Stones/Led Zeppelin rock 'n' roll than any other band on the scene. The boys maintained a busy gigging schedule and an enthusiastic following, but it was a stroke of fortune that helped to set them out in a big way. A young A&R man named Tom Zutaut—who had signed mega-successful Mötley Crüe to Elektra—had taken a job with David Geffen at Geffen Records (the same man who'd employed Slash's father as a cover artist). His mission was to find a band like the Crüe for Geffen—a hard rock or heavy metal group with the same potential for big-time sales and chart-topping hits. When Zutaut found Guns, the wheels were set in motion. By March of 1986, Zutaut had the band under contract and the boys in the studio.

December 1986 saw the release of Guns N' Roses' first album, an EP titled *Live?!*@Like a Suicide* on their own Uzi-Suicide label. The four song set was hard-edged, gritty, and punk-influenced in both sound and attitude: fast, loud, no-frills. The album sold very well for an indie release, and Geffen had the boys back in the studio soon after, putting them to work on what would be their first major-label outing, *Appetite for Destruction*. Producer Mike Clink helped Guns create a tighter, stadium-ready sound in the tradition of idols like Zep, Aerosmith, and the Who—the band churned out strong songs that combined head-banging intensity with memorable melodies and unpredictable mood swings. *Appetite* was a huge success. Nearly a year after its July 1987 release, it hit the top spot on the Billboard chart, and it remained within the Top 10 for well over a year. The album has continued to sell remarkably well—over 15 million units—

and has become one of the biggest selling band debuts of all time. *Appetite* contains three Top 10 singles: "Welcome to the Jungle" (the theme song for Clint Eastwood's "Dirty Harry" movie *The Dead Pool*), "Sweet Child o' Mine" (a chart-topping single), and "Paradise City" (one of the biggest hits of 1989).

While *Appetite for Destruction* continued to move out of stores at a record pace, the band hit the road and opened for acts like Iron Maiden, Mötley Crüe, Aerosmith, and the Rolling Stones. The band continued its meteoric ascent and *G N' R Lies* hit the stores on November 30, 1988. This follow-up to the band's stunning debut, a compilation of their early EP and four new, acoustic-based songs, was nearly as auspicious as their first album. Guns N' Roses avoided the dreaded "sophomore jinx" and had two records on Billboard's Top 10 list at the same time—a rare feat indeed. *G N' R Lies* also included the single "Patience" which went gold after its release in April 1989.

Fans waited anxiously until September 17, 1991, the day Guns N' Roses released not just one, but two new albums—the complex, multi-faceted *Use Your Illusion I* and *Use Your Illusion II*. The new recordings marked a different direction for the band, one in which straight-ahead, headbanging rock songs coexisted alongside epic ballads, piano and synth-driven art rock, acoustic slide blues, horn sections, strings, and back-up vocalists. The *Use Your Illusion* albums quickly became unparalleled successes, landing in the top slots on the charts in not only the U.S. but also Japan, England, Australia, and New Zealand. Arnold Schwarzenegger's blockbuster movie *Terminator 2—Judgement Day* used "You Could Be Mine" as its theme song, turning it into a gold single. Others soon followed, including "Pretty Tied Up (The Perils of Rock N' Roll Decadence)," "November Rain," "Don't Cry," and choice covers of "Live and Let Die" and "Knockin' on Heaven's Door" (used in the movie *Days of Thunder*). The band hit the road in support of the records—as if they needed it—making the *Get in The Ring* tour their first as headliners. That trip was quickly followed by the *Skin and Bones* tour that began in 1992 and ran through the following year. In 1993 G N' R relesed *The Spaghetti Incident?*, a collection of classic punk covers.

Guns N' Roses' membership has undergone quite a few changes since the early '90s. During the *Use Your Illusion* era, former Cult drummer Matt Sorum replaced Steven Adler, and keyboardist Dizzy Reed joined. Izzy Stradlin left in 1991 and was replaced by ex–Kill for Thrills guitarist Gilby Clarke. Slash officially left in 1996. Guitarists Robin Finck of Nine Inch Nails and Buckethead (a.k.a. Brian Carroll) joined the Gunners in 2000. Other shifts in personnel have also happened, as well as a shift towards more of an industrial sound, but Guns N' Roses has always managed to survive and thrive due to the persistence of Axl Rose. Throughout it all, the band has ridden the waves of fame and fortune that have deservedly catapulted them to a permanent place in the pantheon of hard rock legends.

In 1999 the Guns N' Roses song "Oh My God" appeared in the soundtrack to the Schwarzenegger film *End of Days*, and the two-disc *Live Era '87–'93* was released. In August 2002, the band in its latest incarnation—consisting of Axl Rose; Buckethead, Robin Finck, and Richard Fortus on guitars; Dizzy Reed and Chris Pitman on keyboards; Primus drummer Brian "Brain" Mantia; and Replacements bassist Tommy Stinson—played the Hong Kong Convention & Exhibition Center, kicking off their latest multi-national tour. Later that month, they played the 2002 MTV Video Music Awards, where talk centered on their latest project, *Chinese Democracy*.

Guns Gear—Inside the Sounds

Guns N' Roses was never overly infatuated with special effects or fancy signal processing. Opting instead for a more traditional, straightforward, classic rock sound, the guitarists' choices of instruments, amps, and tones set them apart from the pack in the increasingly gaudy, overly slick metal scene of late 1980s Los Angeles. Izzy Stradlin plied many of his indispensable rhythm guitar parts on either of two Gibson ES-175 hollow-body electrics (with cherry and tobacco sunburst finishes)—unusual and eclectic axes for a hard rock player. The selection was largely influenced by blues rocker George Thorogood. Izzy chose a MESA/Boogie Mark III Simuclass head for the recording studio (a fabulous amp), running it though a 4x12 cabinet with Celestion speakers on the top and Electro-Voices on the bottom. He has professed a fondness for Carvin amplifiers as well.

Slash, lead guitarist and outstanding solo voice of the band, has undergone a lengthy equipment odyssey that began in his teenage years and culminated in gear choices that reflect his influences and love of classic rock 'n' roll. After a tenuous beginning, struggling to pick out riffs on a one-string acoustic, Slash acquired copies of classic Gibson designs—the Explorer and the Les Paul. Influenced by the playing and appearance of Aerosmith's Joe Perry and his B.C. Rich Mockingbird, he saved his money and bought himself a mahogany neck-through-body model with Bill Lawrence pickups. A job at an L.A. music store allowed him to acquire a few real classics, including a '59 Fender Strat, a '69 Les Paul "Black Beauty," and a "killer" Fender Twin Reverb combo tube amp. Like many young players, Slash struggled to find the sounds in his ears and imagination, moving away from the vintage classics and back to B.C. Rich, making its Warlock model his primary ax around the time of Guns N' Roses' inception. That guitar was sold when Slash landed an endorsement deal from Jackson, which fit him up with a tremolo-equipped Firebird model he had adorned with a replica of his famous skull-and-top-hat tattoo. Despite his changes, he discovered upon close examination in the studio (where he was busy preparing to record tracks for *Appetite for Destruction*) that his guitar sound still fell well short of the tonal mark he imagined. Producer/engineer Mike Clink then found Slash a yellow, flame-top 1959 Les Paul, an acquisition he later characterized as a "delivery from God." A love affair was born, and when the guitar was run through a cranked 100-watt Marshall head, Slash knew he'd found the sound he'd been dreaming of—the traditional, no-frills, massive tone of idols like Led Zeppelin's Jimmy Page. As Slash's now-immense guitar collection grew, more Les Pauls were added, each equipped with the same Seymour Duncan Alnico II pickups. Among the more than 50 axes he currently owns are other vintage Pauls with classic Gibson PAF ("patent applied for") pickups, customized ESPs, Strats, Charvels, Dobros, a Music Man guitar formerly owned by the Rolling Stones' Keith Richards, and a variety of steel- and nylon-string acoustics.

During the *Appetite for Destruction* sessions, Slash used a vintage Marshall 100-watt head with a 4x12 Marshall half-stack, and a 100-watt Marshall Jubilee half-stack. The *Use Your Illusion* sessions found Slash using a different, vintage Marshall 100-watt head, an amp that has since found a permanent home in the recording studio. On the road, he divides his sound between two 100-watt Jubilee full-stacks (one clean, one dirty) with another two full-stacks onstage as backups. Slash occasionally uses a Dean Markley talk-box played through a separate amp onstage to create intriguing, vocalized effects. Other gear includes four custom-made wah-wahs (built by Matt Bacchi of Oakland's EMB Audio), a Boss seven-band graphic equalizer, and an octave divider (used on the "Paradise City" solo). Slash prefers the heaviest picks he can find, Jim Dunlop Purple Tortex, Ernie Ball .010 strings (the same make and gauge used by Izzy Stradlin), and a Nady 1200 wireless system for unlimited onstage mobility.

While it's certainly illuminating to investigate specific guitars or amps used by Slash, Izzy, or any other personal favorite, it's important to remember that tone is still largely a product of the player, not the equipment. Slash's ultimate gear choices were guided by unique tastes, developed through years of listening, playing, and searching. Your sound will always be impacted by the quality and condition of your equipment, but your technique—the ability to execute your ideas cleanly—pick attack, ears, and personal influences will remain the primary shaping forces of your tone. There are lessons to be learned from Slash's quest for his ideal sound: be patient, be discriminating, be open to change. Save your money for proven, reliable, quality gear and try not to be swayed by flavor-of-the-month fads. Gibson, Fender, Marshall, MESA/Boogie, new or vintage—these names have always stood for the best in classic, authoritative sound. Keep in mind that you or I could step onstage tomorrow with Slash's very own equipment and still not be able to reproduce his trademark tones. We learn a lot through emulation and imitation, but in the end, we still sound like ourselves—which is all for the best, anyway. The point of a book like this is not to help you turn yourself into a Slash clone. Rather, it is hoped that by examining and enjoying the music within, you'll find licks, ideas, and inspiration to aid in your journey towards a unique and successful guitar style that's yours alone. To thine ownself be true—never forget it.

A Glimpse into Slash's Solo Style

Saul Hudson—a.k.a. Slash—is an exciting soloist whose style is both contemporary and firmly rooted in the tradition of past rock guitar masters. With a melodic, blues-based approach, Slash carries the mantle of a guitar continuum that spans the decades from Les Paul, to Jimi Hendrix, to more immediate influences such as Jimmy Page and Jeff Beck. Like all of these players, his solos begin with the blues, then get filtered through his personal musical sensibilities to create something new and uniquely his own. Slash's playing, both live and on recordings, also reflects an uncommon sensitivity to both the song and the listener. Never the ego-tripping shred maniac, he plays with the passion, restraint, and patience reflective of innate musical maturity.

That said, there are a variety of approaches Slash takes to create the memorable, structured solos examined in this book. His toolbox is loaded with familiar techniques and tricks of the trade: legato hammer-ons and pull-offs, extensive string bending, artificial harmonics, slides, muting, and the like. (These techniques are essential to most rock guitar styles, and it is strongly suggested that you familiarize yourself with all of them. A lack of space prevents detailed discussion of them here, but the information at the end of this book is a good place to start.) Much like his strongest influences, Slash is primarily a scale-based soloist, drawing from a small but essential group of scales out of which he spins his melodic ideas. For the many minor key sections in which he solos, the choices are usually the minor pentatonic scale, the blues scale, the Dorian and Aeolian modes, and sometimes the harmonic minor scale. During major key solo sections, Slash plays from the major and minor pentatonic scales, which are frequently supplemented by notes from the blues scale, creating that major-minor sound heard so often in blues.

In the examples that follow, each scale is shown with at least two fingerings and then followed with a lick from a Slash solo in which it is applied. Bear in mind that for every phrase, there are often at least a half dozen fingering possibilities—frequently many more. Make every effort to learn the following scales in as many keys and fingerings as possible. Like many strong rock soloists, Slash can play both inside and outside the "box;" during a G minor solo, for example, he might play from the G blues scale at the 3rd fret, or an octave higher at the 15th, but he isn't confined there. He may approach the scale from the 10th fret of the A string, or the 5th fret of the D string. The deeper your understanding of the neck, the easier it will be for you to express the ideas you hear in your head.

The major scale provides the foundation, melodically and harmonically, for much of what we hear in Western music. Learn it in all keys and neck positions. The pentatonic major scale, shown below in G, is similar, but omits the 4th and 7th degrees of the scale (F and B in the key of C, C and F♯ in the key of G). Slash frequently adds the flat 3rd and flat 5th to these scales as bluesy chromatic passing tones.

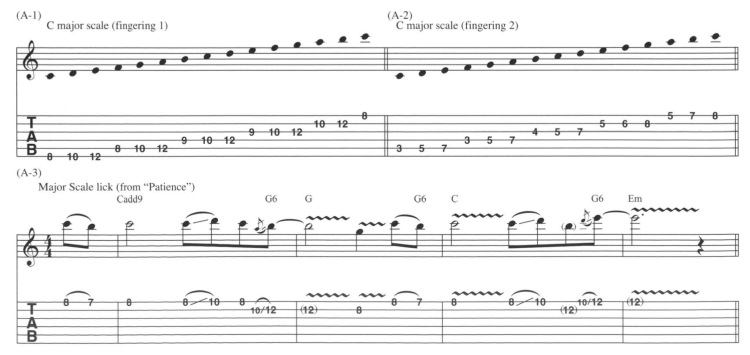

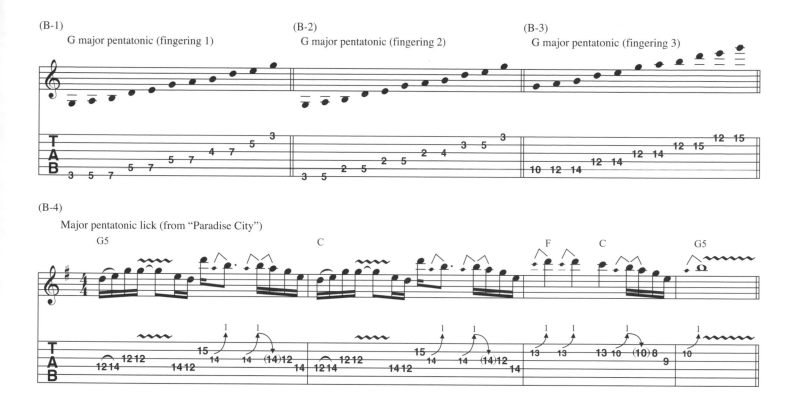

(B-1) G major pentatonic (fingering 1)

(B-2) G major pentatonic (fingering 2)

(B-3) G major pentatonic (fingering 3)

(B-4) Major pentatonic lick (from "Paradise City")

The two scales that follow, the minor pentatonic and blues scales, are doubtless the most frequently heard sounds in rock guitar. Like Slash, learn to play them in both the "box" positions shown below and in as many other places on the neck as you can. There's limitless potential for bending licks here, with Slash most often bending the flat 3rd up to the 4th, the 4th up a whole step or a half step, and the flat 7th up a whole step to the root.

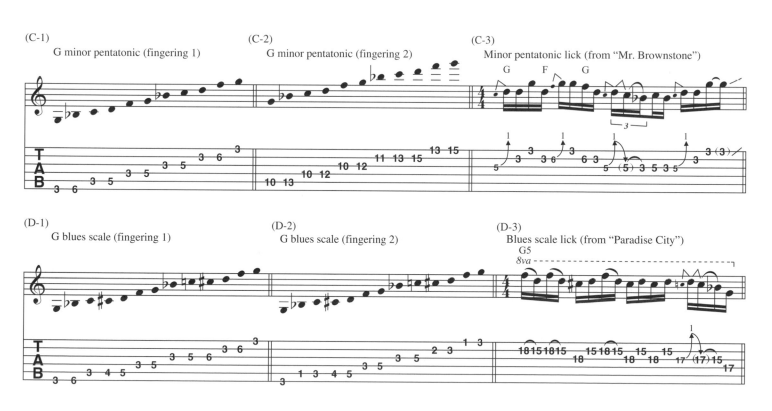

(C-1) G minor pentatonic (fingering 1)

(C-2) G minor pentatonic (fingering 2)

(C-3) Minor pentatonic lick (from "Mr. Brownstone")

(D-1) G blues scale (fingering 1)

(D-2) G blues scale (fingering 2)

(D-3) Blues scale lick (from "Paradise City")

A Glimpse into Slash's Solo Style *Cont.*

Slash uses the modes that follow in minor key solos throughout this book, often in conjunction with notes from the blues or pentatonic minor scales. The Dorian mode is built from the 2nd degree of the major scale (E Dorian contains the same notes as D major); the Aeolian mode (the natural minor scale) is built from the 6th degree of the major scale (C Aeolian contains the same notes as E♭ major). The actual difference between the isolated modes is slight—the former includes a major 6th, the latter, a minor 6th. Notice here and throughout the examples in this book just how much of a difference in sound one note can make.

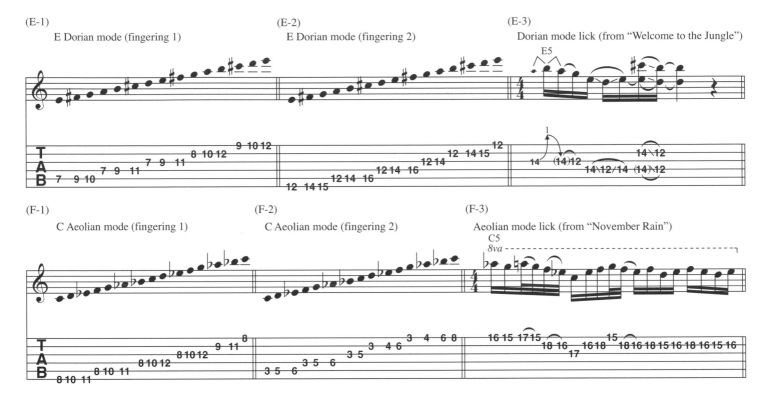

What's shown above is by no means the limit of Slash's soloing approach. Other scales and modes crop up here and there, most notably the harmonic minor scale (identical to the Aeolian mode, but with a natural rather than flat 7th) and Mixolydian mode (similar to a major scale, but with a flat 7th). While in Slash's playing it's not always evident what's cerebral and what's intuitive, all players can benefit from further study of chord-scale relationships (and there are numerous excellent books on the subject). Never be afraid to learn more about your instrument and the way music is constructed in general. Contrary to popular opinion, study won't sap the emotion from your music. If you play honestly and from the heart, new scales and modes will merely be additional colors on a richer tonal palette.

Welcome to the Jungle

from **Appetite for Destruction**

Words and Music by
W. Axl Rose, Slash, Izzy Stradlin,
Duff McKagan and Steven Adler

One of their most popular songs, "Welcome to the Jungle" was one of three Top 10 singles to emerge from *Appetite for Destruction*. This debut hit appeared on the soundtrack of the Clint Eastwood movie *The Dead Pool*, helping to push *Appetite* all the way to #1 on the U.S. charts. This sordid, angry tale of crime and corruption in the big city got heads banging and announced the arrival of a major new force in the world of hard-edged, uncompromising rock 'n' roll.

Intro

The excerpt below includes the parts played by both Slash and Izzy Stradlin. Guitar 1 begins with an interesting palm-muted figure in 16th notes. Simply rest the bottom of your palm gently on the strings near the bridge to create the muffled effect. Each of the first eight measures is actually a steady stream of 16th notes broken up into four three-note phrases and one four-note phrase ("123-123-123-123-1234"), creating shifting, unpredictable accents. The notes in parentheses are *ghost notes* (notes that are more implied than played outright). Listen to the example to hear how the phrase should be played, and try to give the "ghosted" notes a less emphatic pick attack than the others. Guitar 2 has a fairly simple solo melody filled with the types of rock guitar articulations you'll see throughout this book—hammer-ons, slides, and bends. At the end of the Intro, Guitar 1 crunches on a palm-muted B5 chord, while Guitar 2 plays a bluesy lick in eighth notes. Begin the second measure of this phrase by using your ring finger to push the B string up a half step while your pinky plays the As on the 5th fret of the high E string.

TRACK 02
Full Band

TRACK 03
Slow Demo

Welcome to the Jungle *Cont.*

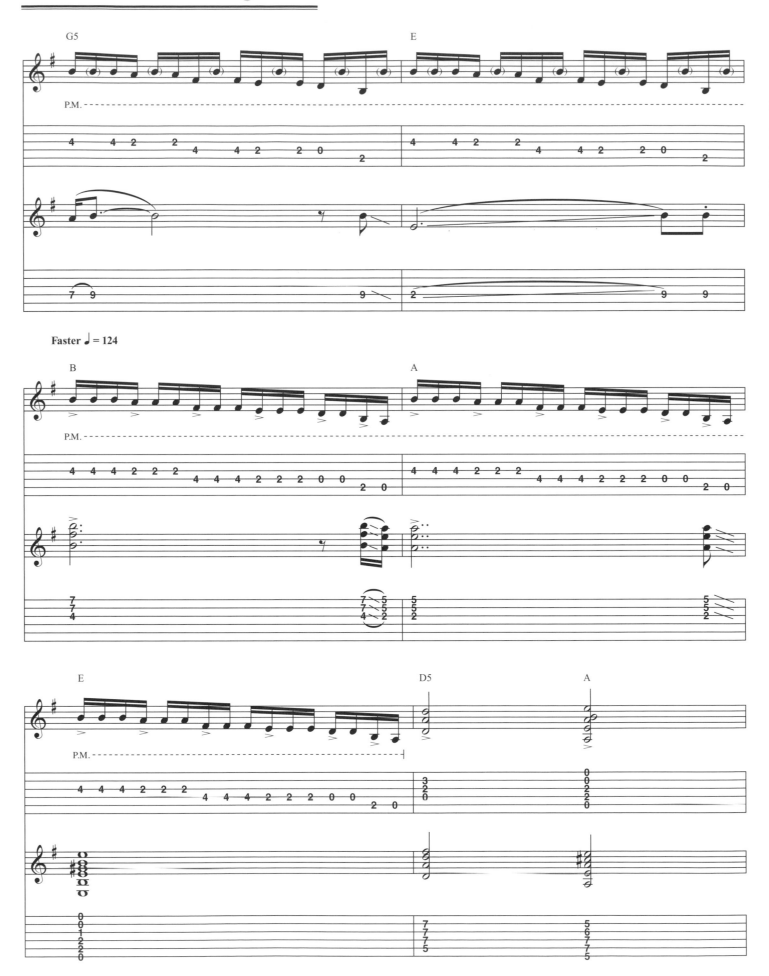

Verse Riff

Here's the riff that sets up and continues during the Verse. Once again, both guitar parts are shown. Check out the way they're arranged to get the most out of two instruments, with similar, interlocking riffs that play off each other and raise the head-banging quotient more than a few notches. The part played by Guitar 1 makes use of open strings and very selective palm muting. Play the part with your index finger barring the G and D strings at the 2nd fret, leaving your middle finger to execute the bent G on the 3rd fret of the low E string. Guitar 2 features power chords on the two bottom strings (fret with your index and ring fingers) before breaking off into a blues-inflected 16th note line in the final measure. Begin the line with your ring finger executing the artificial harmonic at the 7th fret of the G string. Artificial harmonics are created by striking a given note with the edge of your thumb and/or index fingertip at the same time as the pick. This technique may take some practice, but it is an indispensable tool in your rock guitar arsenal. The slide towards the end of the 16th note line should be executed by your index finger.

TRACK 04
Full Band

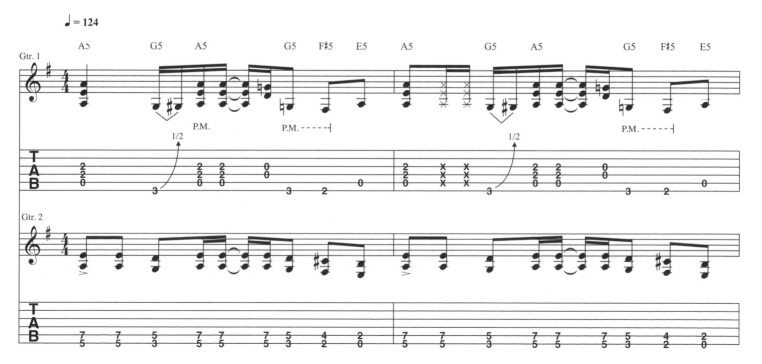

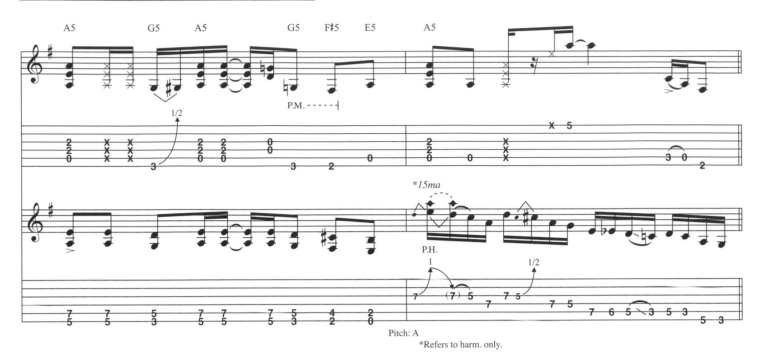

Pitch: A
*Refers to harm. only.

Chorus

For the first two measures of the excerpt below, use your ring finger to barre the D and G strings while your index finger descends on the A string. The final two notes in each measure, played on the low E string, should be fretted by your ring and index fingers. Use your index finger to begin each of the final four measures of the example. You'll need to shift quickly so that your index finger can take the D on the 5th fret of the A string before your middle finger takes on the 5th and 6th frets of the low E.

TRACK 05
Full Band

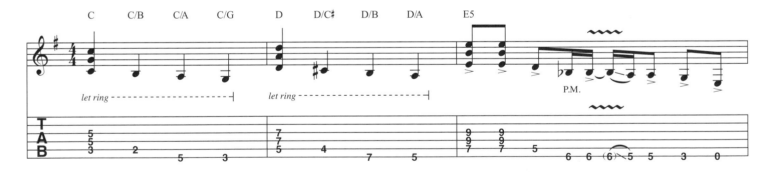

First Solo

This Solo is chock full of classic rock guitar techniques and phrases—and it just begins to scratch the surface of Slash's extensive blues vocabulary. Beginning with a strong, four-bar phrase in *double stops* (two-note chords) the Solo spins off into sliding, bending lines that exhibit a perfect blend of abandon and control. Watch out for the tricky slide at the end of the fourth measure, where you must jump quickly from the 15th fret to the 6th before sliding an entire octave up the G string to the 18th fret. The fifth measure features the first of two over-bends (the second can be found in the final measure, combined with an artificial harmonic)—in each case, the string is pushed up a full step and a half (minor 3rd), necessitating a fair amount of finger strength. Each of these bends should be executed by your ring finger, with your index and middle fingers supplying added strength. Don't neglect to examine the accompanying part played by Guitar 2; it's a fully developed rhythm guitar part that keeps things interesting and provides a rocking launching pad for the Solo. There's a challenging mix of fretted and open string playing, string skipping, slides, and pull-offs that create a honky-tonk piano feel.

TRACK 06
Full Band

TRACK 07
Slow Demo

15

Welcome to the Jungle *Cont.*

Second Solo

Slash's second solo on "Jungle" is full of useful licks and phrases, but is even more remarkable for its sense of organization and strength as a complete statement. The larger lesson here is one of "solo architecture"—the construction of a fundamentally sound statement with a beginning, middle, and end. Whether you are working your own choices out in advance, or have a more improvisational approach (a mixture of the two approaches is generally ideal), you'll likely find that taking a more "structural" approach will lead to richer, more satisfying statements.

At the end of measure 4, use your pinky at the 12th fret of the B string while your ring finger pushes the G string (11th fret) up a whole step. In measure 7, use your index finger to descend the B string while sounding the open high E string; execute the bends in the following measure with your index finger on the G string and your middle finger on the B string.

TRACK 08
Full Band

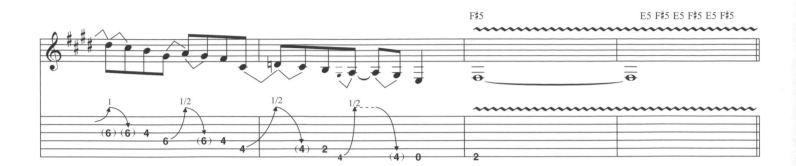

Ending Riff

This short figure apes the phrase at the end of the Chorus before finishing up on an E7#9 chord. The voicing here is fairly tricky, requiring you to barre the B and high E strings with your pinky at the 3rd fret. Make sure to arch your ring finger (on the D string) high enough so you can hear the G# on the first fret of the G string. Don't forget to slowly loosen your low E string as the chord decays for that special, melting-away-into-hell effect.

TRACK 09
Full Band

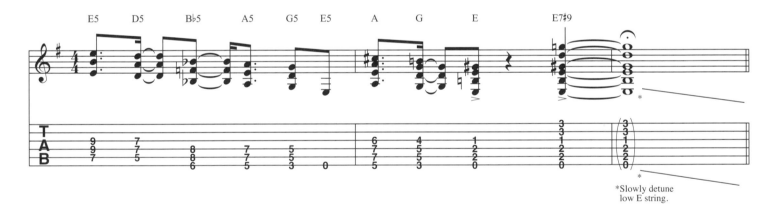

*Slowly detune
low E string.

It's So Easy

from **Appetite for Destruction**

Words and Music by
W. Axl Rose, Slash, Izzy Stradlin, Duff McKagan,
Steven Adler and West Arkeen

This sneering, delightfully arrogant song is pure 1980s rock—lots of attitude and crunching power chords. Beneath it all lies a palpable sense of irony and self-parody, facets that set Guns N' Roses apart from the crowd in 1987. It was never a band that took itself too seriously, and if you can get past the misogynistic bent of the lyrics you'll find a real sense of humor and musical sophistication above and beyond the music of their contemporaries.

Verse Riff

Instead of merely doubling each other, the two guitarists split their parts up to give them a wider tonal range and interlocking rhythmic thrust. The Guitar 1 part should be fretted with your index finger only—barre the D and G strings where indicated and be sure to use an even pick attack so the open strings don't jangle excessively. Guitar 2 begins with power chords thickened by doubling the root an octave higher. Leave your fretting fingers in position in measure 2—you don't need to remove them from the neck, simply dampen the strings with your fingertips.

TRACK 10
Full Band

Chorus Riff

Here's another two-tiered section. Begin the Guitar 1 part with your ring finger barring the B and high E strings at the 5th fret. The Guitar 2 part is very straightforward—use your index finger to barre the D, A, and E strings at the 2nd fret while your middle finger pulls off from A♯ to A♮ on the G string.

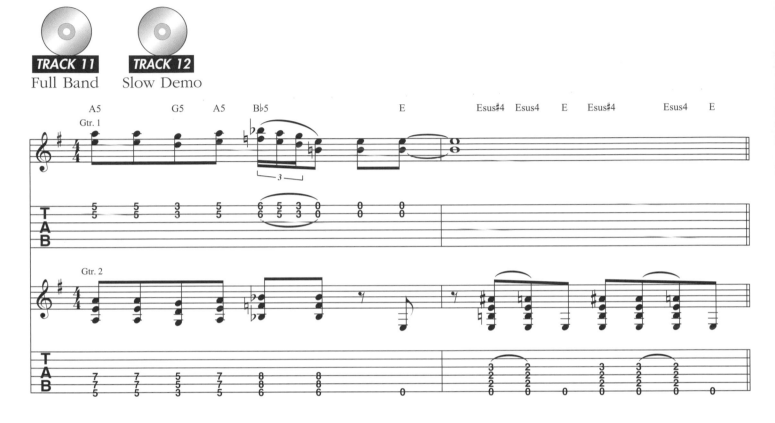

First Solo

Here's a rip-roaring Solo statement that mirrors the out-of-control, hell-bent attitude of the lyrics. Begin with your ring finger, pushing the B string up a full step and a half with the support of your other fingers. Try executing the double bend in measure 2 with your ring finger as well. Instead of barring the two notes, grab the G string as you push the B string up, bending the lower note up a half step. Note that while the whole solo has a distinctly E blues scale feeling (E, G, A, B♭ B♮, D), Slash slips in a few C♯s, lending a Dorian mode (E, F♯, G, A, B, C♯, D) sound to the proceedings.

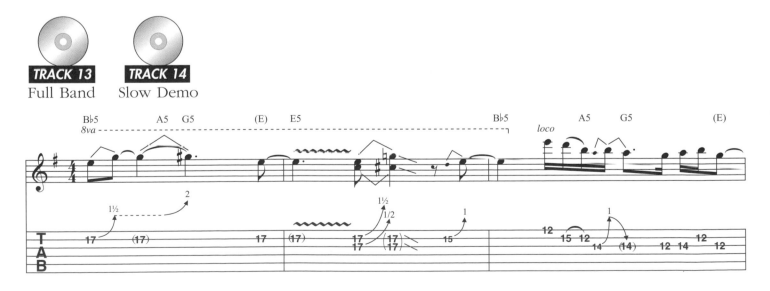

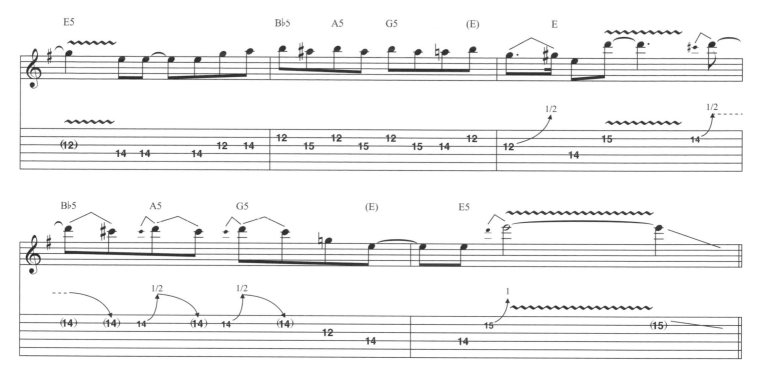

Second Solo

Slash lets it rip over Axl Rose's cry of "It's so easy" as the band vamps out on the riff from the Verse. This Solo is jam-packed with classic rock guitar tricks and techniques, from raked strings (drag your pick over the strings while muffling them slightly until you land on the targeted note) to bends, artificial harmonics, hammer-ons, and pull-offs. In measure 1, use your middle finger on the high E string while your index bends the B string slowly. Slash blends the E blues scale and E Dorian mode to create licks full of fire and melodicism. The key to getting a Solo like this together lies in a slow, patient approach. Don't pick up your axe and expect to sound like Slash right away. Instead, break the Solo down into pieces or phrases, work them over carefully, then add a bit more when you're comfortable. Take your time and slowly work the Solo up to speed. Listen to the recording carefully. Once you've really got it under your fingers, try playing along with Slash.

TRACK 15
Full Band

TRACK 16
Slow Demo

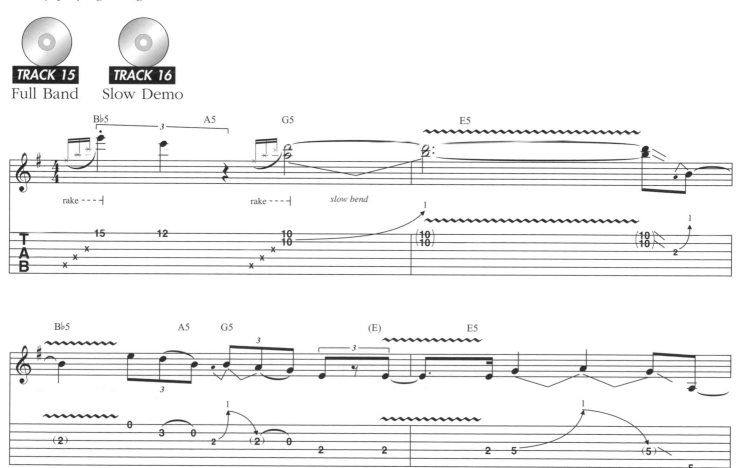

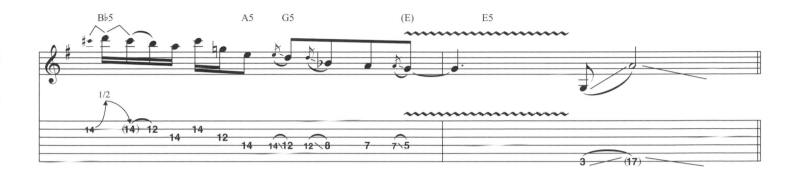

Ending Riff

Begin this phrase with your pinky (or ring finger, if you must)—you'll wind up with your index finger at the 5th fret of the low E string, where you'll have to shift quickly down to the 3rd fret for a bend and pull-off. Don't overlook the slide from a few frets down that begins the phrase, or the palm muting in measures 2, 4, and 6.

TRACK 17
Full Band

Mr. Brownstone

from **Appetite for Destruction**

Words and Music by
W. Axl Rose, Slash, Izzy Stradlin,
Duff McKagan and Steven Adler

Another straight-ahead, rollicking hard rock classic, "Mr. Brownstone" manages to tell a cautionary tale of rock excess without getting too preachy or forgetting that going to extremes can be fun. Lyrically, "Mr. Brownstone" (a.k.a. heroin) begins what would become an ongoing thread for the boys—the life and times of a young band suddenly confronted with immense popularity, overexposure, groupies, toadies, and hangers-on, as well as a number of seriously burgeoning substance abuse problems. One thing you can't say about Guns N' Roses is that they weren't honest!

Intro Riff

The riff below, shown in two parts, sets up the Verse, where it appears again in a pared-down variation; it's also interjected in various places throughout the tune as a sort of short instrumental interlude. Be sure to pay close attention to the various articulations indicated—the Guitar 1 part in particular is full of hammer-ons and pull-offs, while Guitar 2 eschews them for a steadier pick attack with occasional palm muting.

TRACK 18
Full Band

TRACK 19
Slow Demo

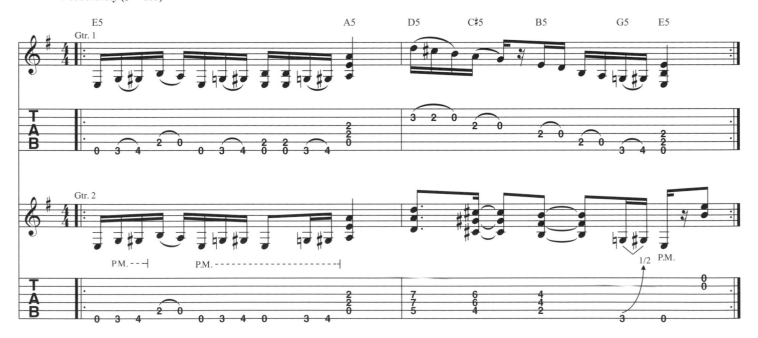

24

Chorus

This section begins with shifting barre chords before breaking down into single-note lines in measure 4. Begin that measure with your middle finger on the A string (5th fret). Shift your hand up for the final four notes of the measure, so that your index and ring fingers take the hammered-on notes on the D and G strings. Watch out for the details in the final four measures, including hammer-ons, vibrato, and bends. Begin the line in the final measure with your ring finger; use your index finger for the D, C♯, and B on the A string and your middle finger for the Gs on the 3rd fret of the low E string.

TRACK 20
Full Band

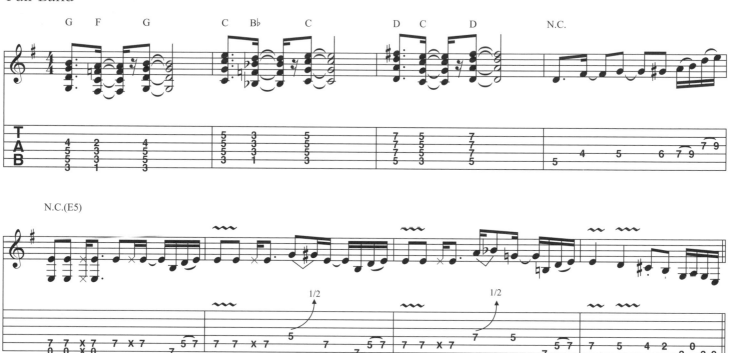

Solo

Slash stands out from the pack with his ability to create Solos full of passion and excitement while never losing a sense of structure and organization. Here he spins off a real scorcher that pushes the limits but never dissolves into chaos. Check out the call-and-response phrasing in the beginning—measures 1 and 3 each contain similar ideas that are answered by faster lines in measures 2 and 4. The bend that begins the Solo should be played with your index finger on the high E string (14th fret) while your ring finger pushes the B string (17th fret) up a whole step to match it. The triplets in measure 2 should be executed by your ring finger, pulling off to your index finger from the 16th to the 14th fret. Check out the over-bend in measure 5, where the A on the B string (22nd fret—the top fret on most fingerboards) is pushed up a major 3rd to C; use your ring finger, backed up by your index and middle fingers, to execute the bend. The measures that follow contain a number of fast, difficult licks that should be worked up very slowly. Don't overlook the details—bends, slides, hammer-ons, pull-offs—and be patient. The final four measures of the Solo are simpler and follow a chord progression similar to that of the song's Chorus. Slash spins off some classic blues licks that follow the chords up the neck before finishing off with a series of unison bends played by the index and ring fingers on the high E and B strings, respectively.

TRACK 21 Full Band

TRACK 22 Slow Demo

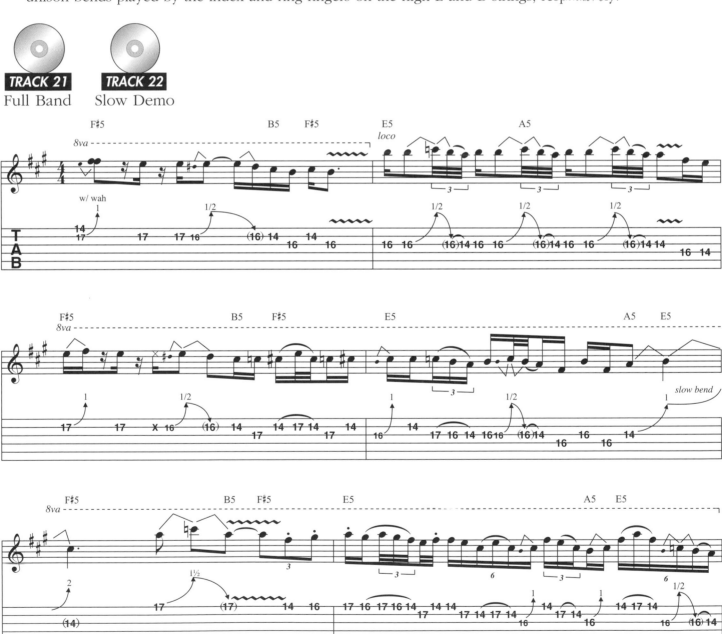

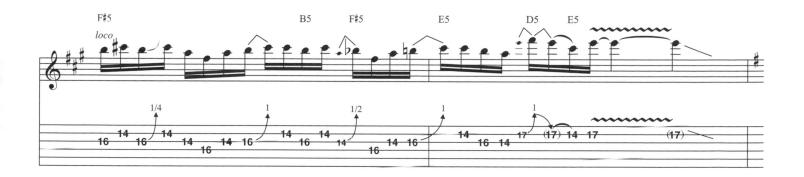

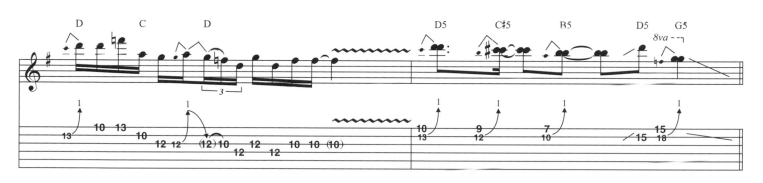

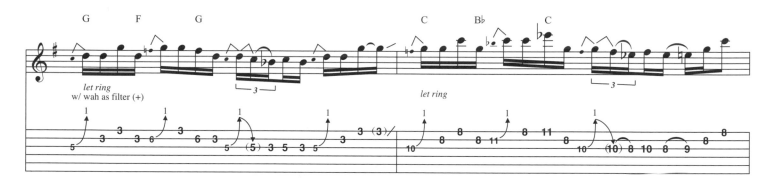

Outro Riff

This easy lick begins with the twin guitars of Slash and Izzy split an octave apart before coming together in unison towards the end. The higher part can be played with either your ring finger or pinky on the 7th fret of the A string. Don't shy away from the pinky if you're not used to using it much—take this opportunity to start working it in. The rest of the example should be fairly obvious—watch out for pull-offs and palm muting where indicated, and for the artificial harmonic in measure 2.

TRACK 23 Full Band

TRACK 24 Slow Demo

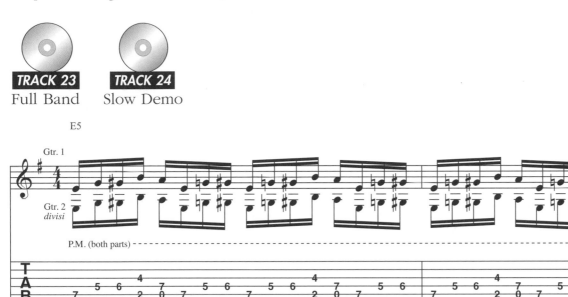

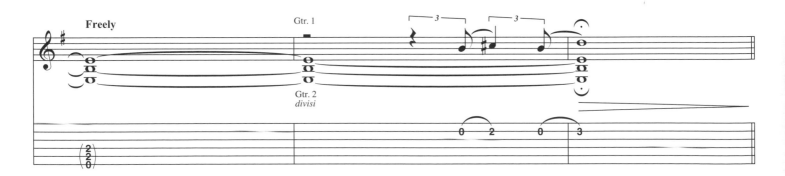

Paradise City

from **Appetite for Destruction**

Words and Music by
by W. Axl Rose, Slash, Izzy Stradlin,
Duff McKagan and Steven Adler

The second of the three smash hits from *Appetite for Destruction*, "Paradise City" combines an anthem-like Chorus, acoustic chord playing, furious metal riffing, and escapist lyrics to create a memorable song. Slash's classic riffs and solos helped put "Paradise City" on the Billboard charts and made it one of the most memorable tunes of the 1980s.

Intro Chords

A clean, crisp sound gets "Paradise City" started. Let the individual notes of each chord ring for their full durations as this catchy progression sets the tone, barely hinting at the metal mayhem to come. Use your middle and ring fingers (on the G and D strings, respectively) to execute the double hammer-on at the start of measure 3 while your index finger takes the C on the 1st fret of the B string. Your pinky should play all the Gs on the 3rd fret of the high E string during the 2nd and 3rd measures.

TRACK 25
Full Band

TRACK 26
Slow Demo

Intro Melody

This tuneful lick paraphrases the song's Chorus. Begin the phrase with your index finger at the 12th fret of the D string and use your ring finger to execute the bends on the G string. The same finger should bend the B string (13th fret) in measure 3 before shifting down to perform the whole step bend at the 10th fret. Be sure to include the indicated hammer-ons and vibrato.

TRACK 27
Full Band

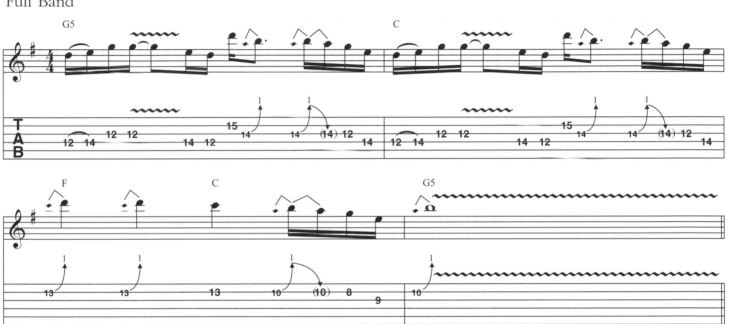

Verse

Heads bang furiously when this heavy, hard-driving riff kicks into gear, and the contrast with the earlier, gentler sections makes it even more effective. The palm-muted, parallel power chords on the A and low E strings move by fairly quickly, so you may want to practice this riff slowly before taking it up to tempo. Each G5 chord in the example should get some quick finger vibrato as well. The riff repeats in a pared-down, single line version in the latter half of the excerpt as Axl Rose's vocal enters. For the final measure, pick the first note once (C on the 3rd fret of the A string), bend it up a half step, release it, then pick the 4th note (B♭ on the 1st fret). As the G on the low E string rings out, slide quickly up and down the neck on the final beat of the measure.

TRACK 28
Full Band

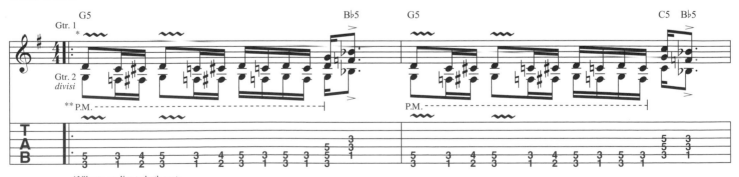

*Vibrato applies to both parts.
**Palm muting applies to both parts.

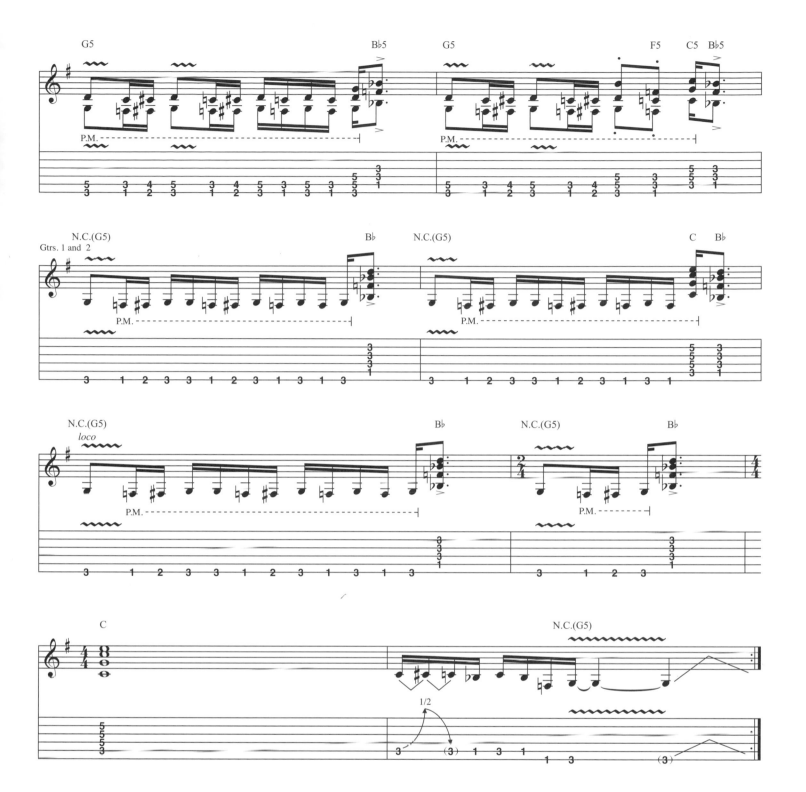

Solo

This eight-measure Solo is actually divided into two sections: four measures revolving around the song's main riff in G (taken from the G blues scale) in which Slash uses an octave divider pedal to create wickedly thick lines, and then a second section which begins in A before shifting back down to G. Slash removes the octaver and adds a wah pedal for this section. The end of the excerpt overlaps into the next section of the song. Try bending the second note of the example—F on the D string—up a whole step with your index finger (a bit of a challenge without the other fingers backing it up), which will leave you in good position to catch the 16th notes at the end of the measure. Look ahead to measures 3 and 4. In both, Slash uses an interesting technique wherein he doubles a note on the high E string with the same pitch on the B string played immediately after (F in measure 3, G in measure 4). In the first instance, use your ring finger to bend the G string, then your middle finger on the B string (3rd fret) and your index finger on the high E (1st fret) before sliding your ring finger up the B string to the 6th fret. In the fourth measure, begin with a middle finger bend (5th fret of the G string), before hammering on from your index to middle fingers and landing on the high E string (3rd fret) with your index finger. Finish out the lick by sliding up the B string with your ring finger to the 8th fret.

Measures 5 and 6 find us in classic blues territory. The Solo finishes up with double stop bending on the G and B strings, interrupted by raked triplets (barre the 3rd fret). The bends can be fretted with either your middle and ring fingers or with a ring finger barre. Try it both ways; the latter is definitely more difficult, but it may help you to develop vital bending strength.

TRACK 29 **TRACK 30**
Full Band Slow Demo

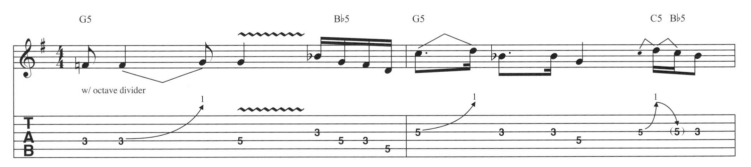

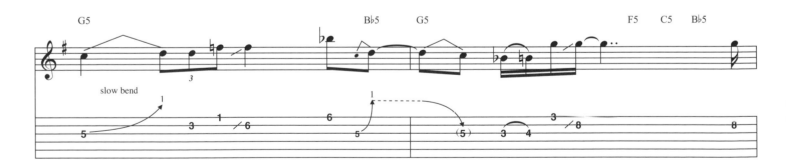

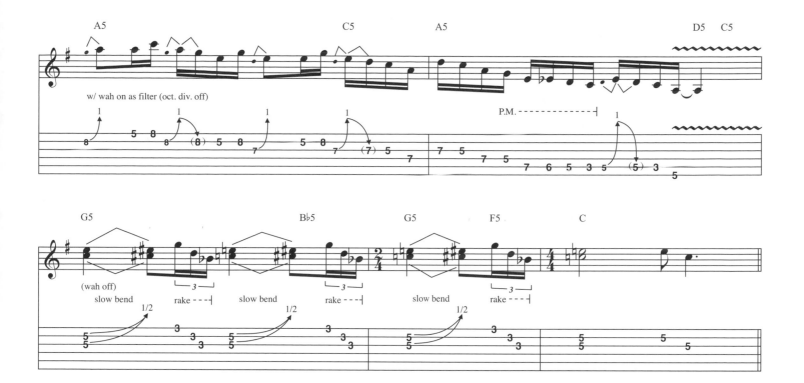

Bridge

This familiar lick moves back and forth between D5 and C5 chords; merely slide down the neck two frets and then back up again. The hammer-ons are from your index to your middle finger; all notes on the high E string should be taken by your index finger alone. This is the kind of catchy little phrase that creeps subconsciously into your own playing and pops out in the middle of something months down the line.

TRACK 31
Full Band

33

Interlude

The section below takes the main riff from the Verse of the tune and puts it into a new guise, with a moving chord progression (taken from the Chorus), double-time feel, and added complexity to the line. The actual playing is fairly straightforward here; watch out for the vibrato, bends, slides, and palm muting. This Interlude serves as a jumping-off point for the song's climax, where Slash solos furiously over Axl's impassioned cry of "Oh, won't you please take me home."

TRACK 32 — Full Band

TRACK 33 — Slow Demo

Outro Solo

Here are more burning riffs and licks from Slash over a repeated, eight-measure chord progression. What's shown below comprises about half of the entire Outro Solo, which is very long and complex, but is nonetheless jam-packed with burning lines that are excellent additions to your soloing arsenal. It's important when tackling long and difficult Solos like this that you work yourself slowly up to speed. Don't try to digest too much at once.

Start off by playing the minor 3rd bends on the B string with your ring finger, using the fingers behind it for added bending strength. The ensuing line, laden with triplets, may take some serious practice at a much slower tempo. A four-measure, repeated triplet phrase follows, giving us a bit of a breather. Measures 13–16 spin off into rapid-fire legato lines taken from the G Dorian mode (G, A, Bb, C, D, E, F), probably the second most common scale (after the blues scale) that you'll find in a Slash solo. The keys to this Solo are the hammer-ons and pull-offs; you'll need them to get the kind of smooth phrasing the line requires. Play the segment slowly, work out the rhythms and fingering, then gradually bring it all up to tempo. After the first 16 measures, Slash slows down a bit, playing mostly eighth note phrases, so the going's a little easier. Check out the tasty melodic idea in measures 33 and 34—a singable, bluesy line that quickly careens back into shredding.

Even in this high-energy environment, he manages to build an exciting and intelligent Solo full of contrasts and astonishing rhythmic accuracy. Slash's bursts of speed are never chaotic or careless; rather, they are controlled, musical, and technically sound. The excerpt below ends with a long and extremely challenging line that stretches out for a full eight measures. Once again, it's chock-full of hammer-ons and pull-offs, and, while fairly straightforward rhythmically, fingering issues and the need for sheer chops should make it a challenge for even the most experienced player.

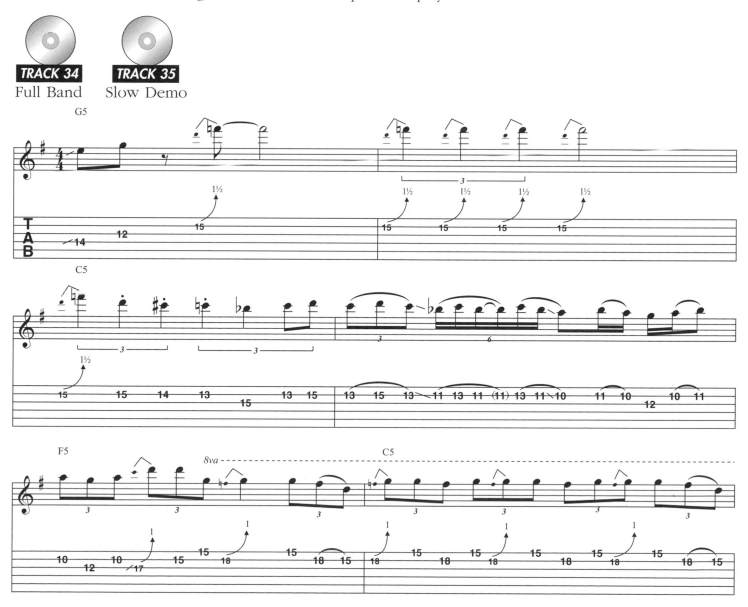

TRACK 34
Full Band

TRACK 35
Slow Demo

35

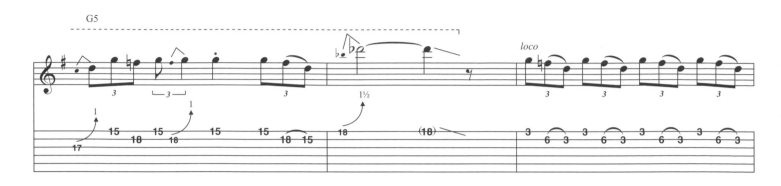

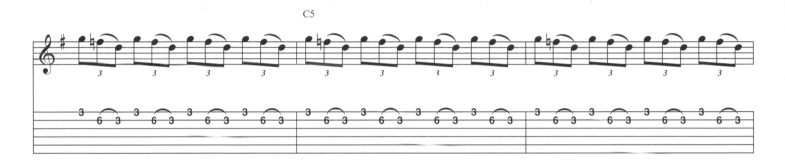

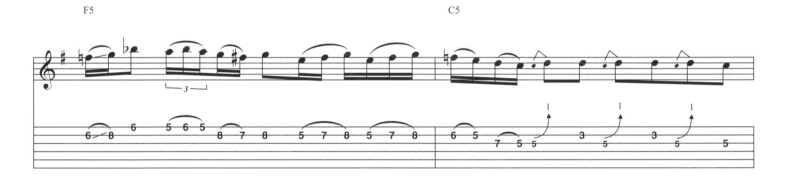

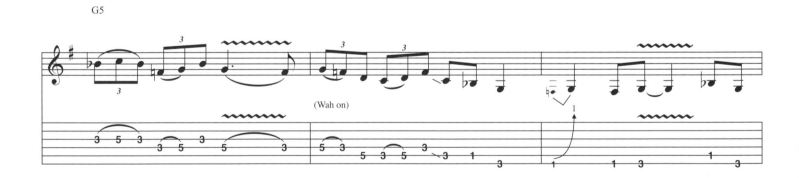

Paradise City *Cont.*

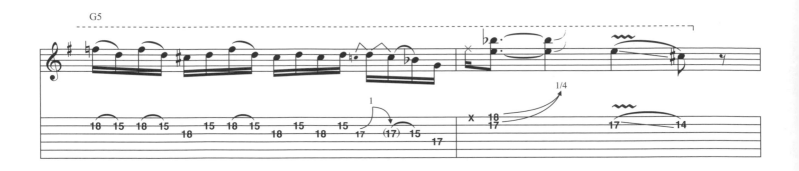

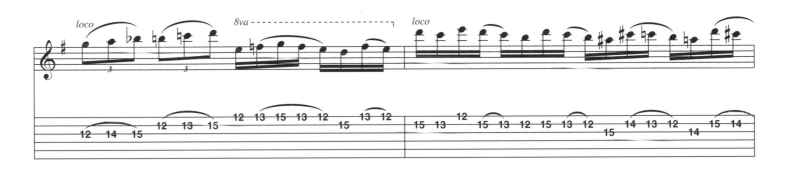

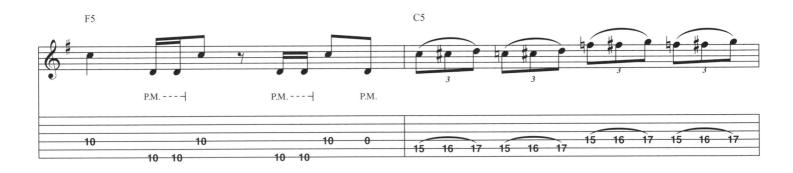

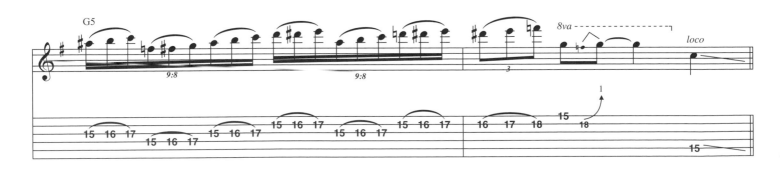

My Michelle

from **Appetite for Destruction**

Words and Music by
W. Axl Rose, Slash, Izzy Stradlin,
Duff McKagan and Steven Adler

After a provocative acoustic Intro, "My Michelle" kicks into gear with tight metal riffs and screeching vocals from Axl Rose. The song is another perfect example of the band's skill in constructing multi-faceted hard rock with memorable melodies and brutally honest lyrics reflecting the sleazy world in which they moved.

Verse Riff

This slick riff is full of menacing, head-banging intensity. Use alternate picking (beginning with a downstroke) in the first and third measures and the side of your picking hand to create the muffled chords throughout. The first three palm-muted F#5 chords in measure 2 should be played with downstrokes for added impact and heaviness.

TRACK 36
Full Band

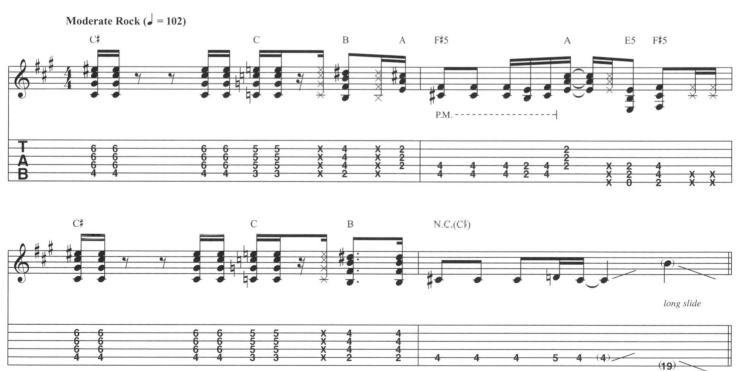

Bridge

Blues and country rock meet heavy metal in this interesting little section. Be sure to use an even-handed pick attack to prevent the open strings from jangling excessively. Use your index finger to execute the slide from the 4th to the 5th fret on the A string in measures 1 and 5, and your middle finger to bend the low E string in measure 3. You might recognize parts of the riff from "Johnny B. Goode"—there's always a little bit of Chuck Berry in every good rock band!

TRACK 37
Full Band

TRACK 38
Slow Demo

Solo

This Solo, constructed almost entirely of bends and effects, is built over a progression that imitates the rhythms of the Verse. Begin the Solo with your index finger at the 7th fret of the high E and B strings before using your ring finger to execute the first bend. The long, slow bend in measure 2 should be played with your middle finger on the G string and ring finger on the B string; it's a difficult bend to play accurately and requires a good deal of finger strength to really nail the pitches. It's a good idea in instances like these (and in the bends that follow on both the G and A strings) to play the pitches you're "targeting" first, and then check to see if your bends are actually matching those pitches. The bend in measure 4 is somewhat out of the ordinary in that it's the A string that is repeatedly pushed up a major 3rd (two whole steps). The bent low E string in measure 6 will have to be fretted by your index finger alone—an additional challenge. Finish up by shifting your hand so that your ring finger executes the first bend and your middle finger the second bend in measure 7; use the ring finger again in the final measure to bend the D string before you play the artificial harmonic with added vibrato.

TRACK 39
Full Band

TRACK 40
Slow Demo

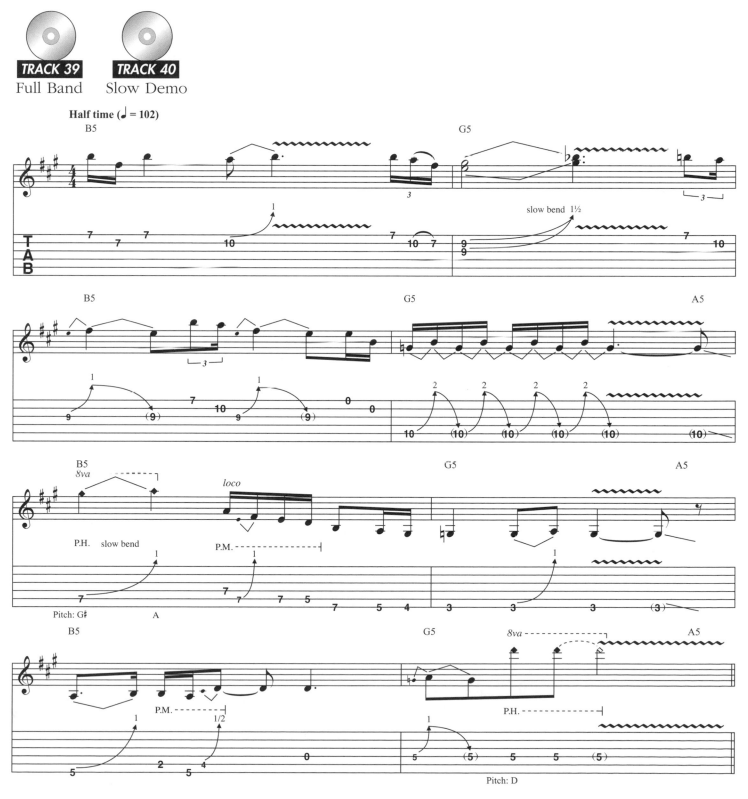

Ending Riff

Here's a little rockabilly riff that's repeated four times before ending up in a series of pull-offs to the open D and G strings. For the repeated measures, use your ring finger to bend the low E string while your index finger barres the D and G strings.

TRACK 41
Full Band

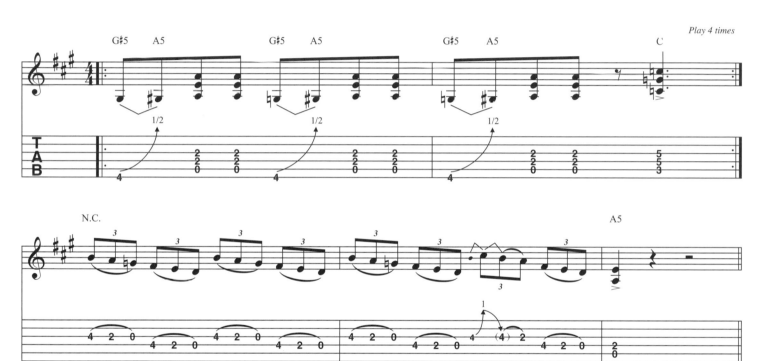

Sweet Child o' Mine

from *Appetite for Destruction*

Words and Music by
W. Axl Rose, Slash, Izzy Stradlin,
Duff McKagan and Steven Adler

The last of the big three from *Appetite for Destruction*, "Sweet Child o' Mine" was the first Guns N' Roses video to get regular airplay on MTV—it also became the band's biggest hit, shooting all the way to the top spot on the Billboard charts in 1988. Slightly gentler than their other big successes, "Sweet Child" nonetheless continued the band's winning formula of acoustic Intros, riff-based hard rock, and memorable melodies.

Intro

The bell-toned eighth note line that begins the song continues as drums, bass, and acoustic guitar join in and really get the groove going. Begin the single-note line with your index finger on the 12th fret of the D string. You'll stay strictly in 12th position for this part—in other words, all notes on the 12th fret will be played by your index finger, all notes on the 14th fret by your ring finger, and all notes on the 15th fret by your pinky. From there, it's merely a matter of getting your picking to be clean and accurate. Listen to the controlled and even way Slash plays the part, and then try it yourself. The accompanying part, played on steel-string acoustic guitar, is simple, folksy, and effective. Use gentle, even strumming and let the chords ring for their full durations while playing the little eighth note phrase that appears in every other measure.

TRACK 42
Full Band

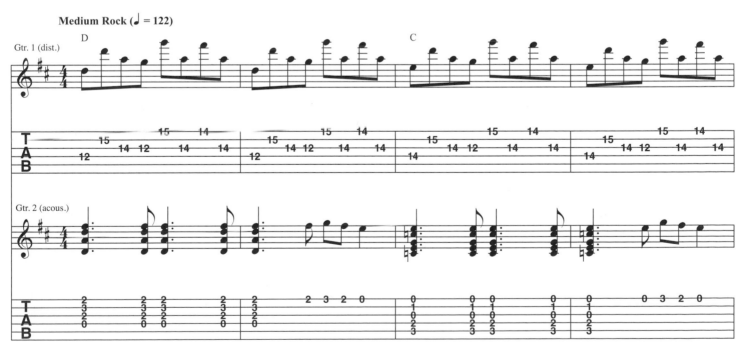

Sweet Child o' Mine *Cont.*

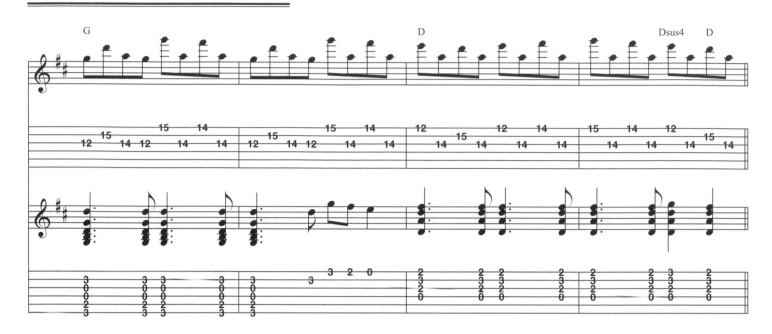

Chorus

The eighth note line returns—with Izzy's distorted power chords in the background—for the song's Chorus. Begin the line with your ring finger barring the D, G, and B strings at the 14th fret. You'll need to shift down for the second measure, using your pinky to begin the line at the 13th fret of the B string. The second half of the excerpt follows the Chorus vocal. Use your index finger to slide down the B string in measure 12; the two bends that follow should be accomplished via your ring finger, while the bent high E string will require a pinky bend. The final bend, on the 9th fret of the G string, should be taken by your middle finger.

TRACK 43
Full Band

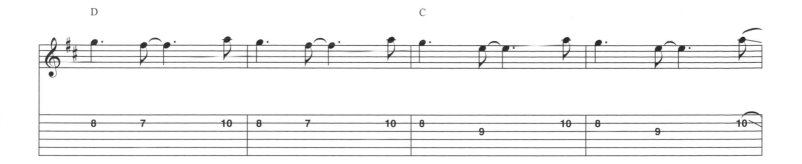

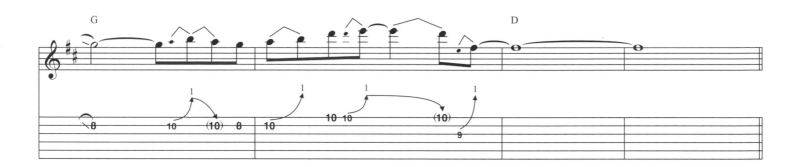

First Solo

This melodic Solo is played over an E minor progression and is constructed mainly of notes taken from the E harmonic minor scale (E, F♯, G, A, B, C, D♯). This may be one of the simpler Solos to play here, technically speaking, but it's also one of the strongest, with clearly defined melodic themes that stay with you long after the song has ended. Once again, the music calls for strong and accurate string bending, so be sure you're really nailing those pitches. As with all of the other examples, practice this slowly before you take it up to speed.

TRACK 44
Full Band

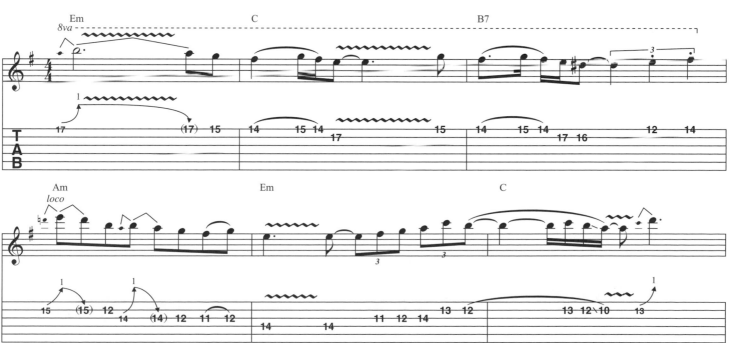

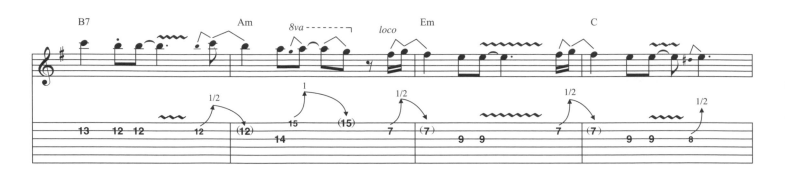

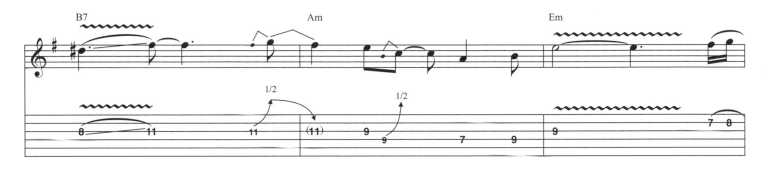

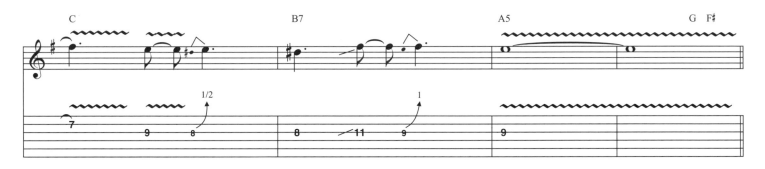

Second Solo

While the first Solo ends on a sustained E, the long line that begins this next Solo creeps in underneath. Slash really raises the song's intensity here, with soulful bends and fiery, blues-inflected lines. The first line is quite difficult, with shifting and sliding hand positions, so be patient and put it together slowly. Play the first slide (measure 2) on the high E string with your pinky (from the 12th to the 14th fret) and the second with your ring finger (14th to 15th fret). The triplet in measure 3 should be performed with your middle finger and your pinky. There are a number of fairly common, blues-style licks that follow, underlining the importance of that influence on Slash. The bends in measures 10 and 11 are good examples. Try bending the G string (14th fret) with your middle finger while barring the B and high E strings with your ring finger (15th fret). The Solo wraps up with a repeated blues line filled with bends on the G and B strings. Use your middle finger for the lower and ring finger for the higher string bends here. An over-bend on the high E string follows, where A on the 15th fret is pushed up a full step and a half to C, before a short line with 16th note triplets dovetails nicely into the next section.

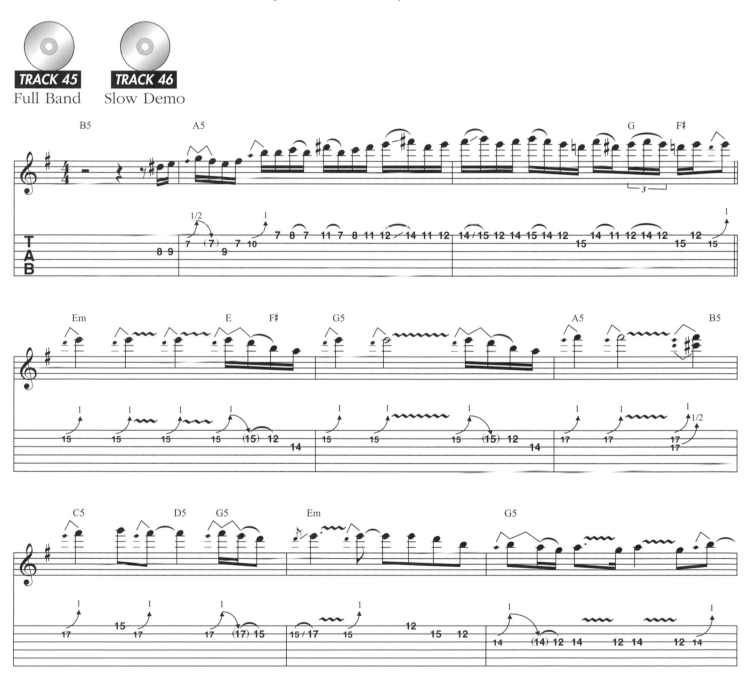

Sweet Child o' Mine *Cont.*

Outro Solo and Ending

Axl Rose's impassioned cries are aided immensely by wailing bends and lines from Slash's Les Paul. There's a series of soaring bends on the high E string before Slash spits out a complex line of repeated quintuplets. Check out the way he uses a repeated, descending, four-note phrase (E, D, B, A) with the five-notes-per-beat rhythm, creating an interesting "across the bar" feeling. To really understand a lick like this, try singing it without your guitar while you beat out the quarter note beat with your hands or feet— it should help you to see exactly where each note falls in relation to the beat. After a series of quarter note triplets and sliding, sustained notes, we descend to the final, open, low E string. While the note decays, place your right hand on the body of your guitar, your left thumb behind its headstock, and push gently in opposite directions with each hand to bend the note down a half step. You can, of course, use a tremolo bar if you have one, but Slash almost always avoids them, favoring instead a number of classic Gibson Les Pauls with floating bridges and stop-bar tailpieces.

TRACK 47
Full Band

TRACK 48
Slow Demo

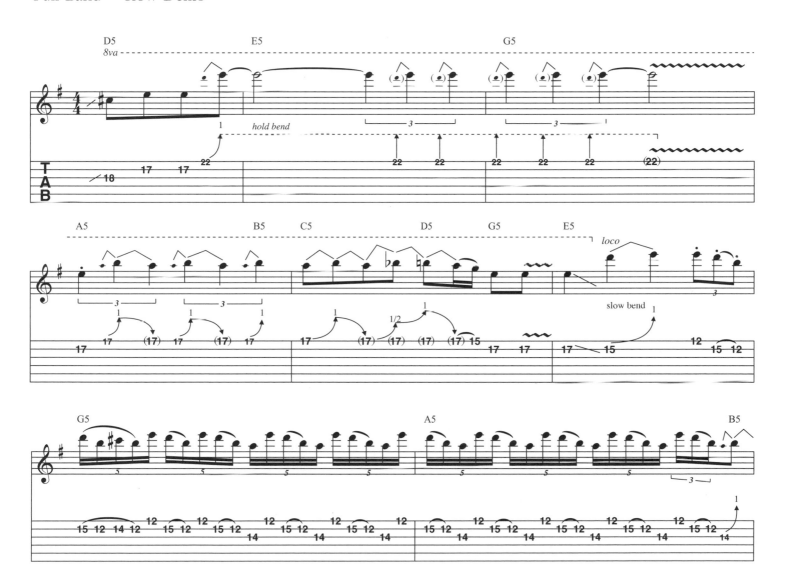

Sweet Child o' Mine *Cont.*

Patience

from G N' R Lies

Words and Music by
W. Axl Rose, Slash, Izzy Stradlin,
Duff McKagan and Steven Adler

Guns N' Roses released *"G N' R Lies"* at the close of 1988, a compilation of four songs from their original 1986 EP (*Live ?!*@ Like a Suicide*) and four entirely new, acoustically-oriented pieces. Among the latter was the gentle rock ballad called "Patience"—a sensitive (some might say sappy) and melodic song catchy enough to break Billboard's top five. Built on a foundation of layered steel-string guitars, it features simple, attractive arpeggio chords and some single-line acoustic soloing by Slash.

Intro

This pretty Introduction unfolds around Axl Rose's lilting, whistled melody. The first eight measures shown here are repeated as "Riff A" during the eight measures that follow; Slash joins in at that point with a melodic, acoustic Solo built of single note lines and country-influenced double stops. The final eight measures of the example return to Guitar 1 for the completion of the Intro. The actual playing is fairly uncomplicated throughout. Guitar 1's chordal accompaniment features some easy hammer-ons, pull-offs, and string-skipping arpeggios, but your biggest challenge is to make the part as clean and pretty as it sounds here. The same goes for the Slash's solo part—try to bring out the line's beauty and simplicity, with accurate bending, sliding, and even tones.

TRACK 49
Full Band

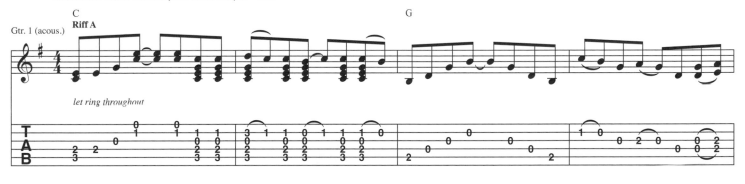

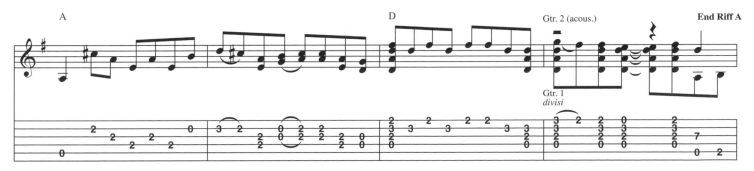

Patience *Cont.*

Verse

The excerpt below includes both guitar parts and is yet another example of the boys' skill at arranging for maximum fullness and effectiveness. Check out how the two parts shift from unison to harmony and back again, providing melodic and rhythmic counterpoint to each other. For Guitar 1, use your pinky to pull off from the 3rd to the 1st fret on the B string in measure 2 and your index finger to grab all notes on the 2nd fret in measure 4. In measure 5 of the Guitar 2 part, place your ring finger on the 7th fret of the D string with your index finger barring the G, B, and high E strings at the 5th fret. Hammer on with your middle finger from the 6th to the 7th fret on the G string and finish up by using your index and middle fingers to fret the final two notes of the measure on the A string.

TRACK 50
Full Band

Chorus

This simple and effective section makes use of pretty, open chords that are alternately strummed and arpeggiated. Use your ring finger to fret the Ds and Bs on the B string in measure 2, your ring and middle fingers to fret the final two notes of measure 3, and your pinky to fret the G on the high E string over the D chord in measure 7.

TRACK 51
Full Band

Solo

Here's another simple and memorable Slash Solo, underlining his blues and country influences. Aside from technical considerations, the lessons here again concern structure, composition, and development of melodic themes. Check out how he returns three times to a simple three-note phrase (C–B–C) at the start of the Solo, and then to bending phrases in measures 9, 10, and 11. Technically, this should be one of Slash's easiest outings to learn, with minimal demands on your fingering and picking chops. In measures 1 and 3, use your middle finger to slide from the 8th to the 10th fret and from the 10th to the 12th fret. Use your index finger for the slides in measures 6 and 7. Your ring finger should do all of the bending in measures 9–13, and take the B string bends beginning in measure 18.

TRACK 52
Full Band

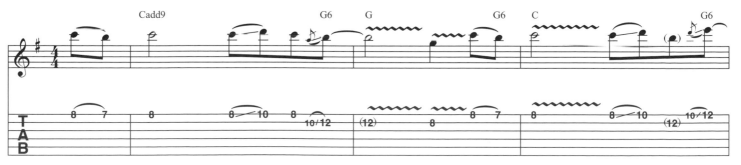

Live and Let Die

from _Use Your Illusion I_

Words and Music by
Paul McCartney and Linda McCartney

Paul and Linda McCartney's classic theme song for the James Bond movie of the same name takes on new life in this inspired, fitting remake. The all-for-yourself, damn-it-all-to-hell sentiment of the lyrics is completely one with the Guns N' Roses attitude, and the music itself combines head-banging intensity with tuneful melodies that make it a perfect cover for the band.

Verse

A fairly straightforward acoustic guitar pattern accompanies the Verse. You can use a pick or play the part fingerstyle, but be aware that if you choose the former, you'll encounter a few difficulties along the way. Notice that in measures 2 and 4 there are instances where two notes are played at once on either the A or D strings plus the high E string. Since it's nearly impossible to play both notes with a pick without sounding the open strings in between, you may want to try picking the lower note while using your ring finger to pluck the higher pitch.

TRACK 53
Full Band

Chorus

This massive Chorus gets its power in part from the dual guitars pounding out heavy, ringing chords—a great contrast to the preceding section. You'll need to use your pinky to fret the high D in measure 2 (7th fret of the G string). Don't omit the scratchy, muted 16th notes that precede most of the chords. The final measure shifts quickly to 3/8—each eighth note in the previous time signature now equals a full beat in the new one. Try counting the shift from 4/4 to 3/8 as "1-and-2-and-3-and-4-and-1-2-3" with both numbers and "ands" being given the same duration.

TRACK 54
Full Band

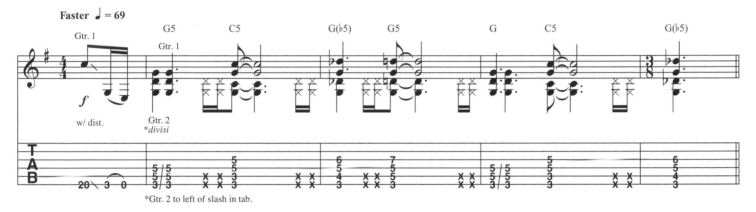

*Gtr. 2 to left of slash in tab.

Interlude Riff

Perhaps the most memorable section of a very memorable tune, this Interlude section should be executed with barres on the D, G, and B strings; your middle finger should not come into play at all during this part. Don't skip the descending slides in every other measure, and be sure to give both open and fretted notes equal weight and volume.

TRACK 55
Full Band

Bridge

The song takes another left turn with this reggae-inspired Bridge. Guitar 2 is Izzy's chordal part—use alternate picking while you strum and keep the side of your right palm against the strings to muffle them where indicated. At the same time, Slash plays some interesting little fills and snippets. Use your middle finger on the G string and ring finger on the high E to play the sliding double stops in the second and third measures.

TRACK 56
Full Band

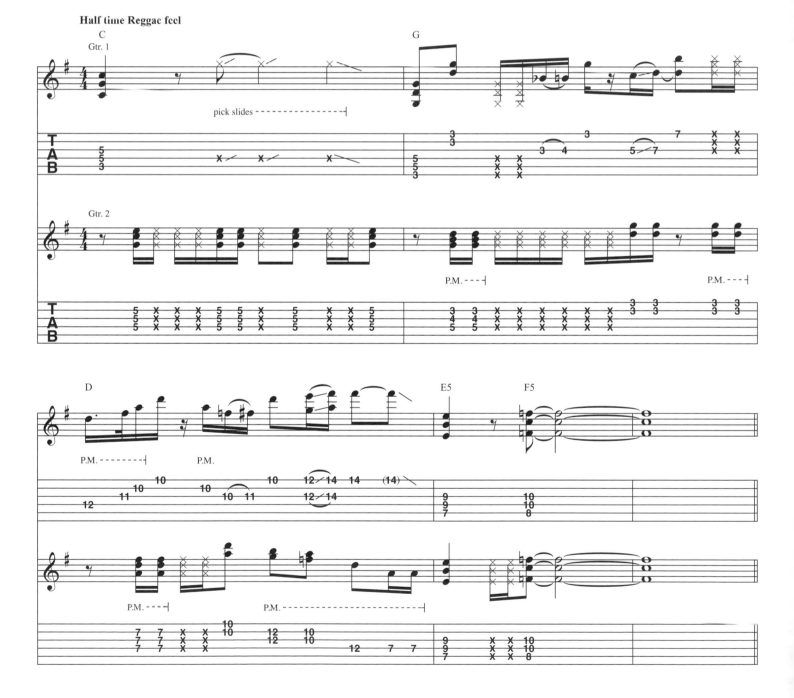

Don't Cry (Original)

from **Use Your Illusion I**

Words and Music by
Izzy Stradlin and W. Axl Rose

"Don't Cry" appeared on both *Use Your Illusion I* and *II*, with identical music and original and alternate lyrics, respectively. The song is typical Guns N' Roses balladry—acoustic Intros, gradually increasing heaviness, catchy Chorus hooks, and smoldering solos from Slash. "Don't Cry" stands out a bit from other Guns ballads because of the depth and honesty of its emotion—compare it to say, "Patience," from two years prior—and for its heavily layered, complex, and polished production. The song became one of a number of chart-toppers from the *Illusion* albums, helping Guns N' Roses to achieve the rare feat of having both the number one and number two records in the country simultaneously.

Verse

The excerpt below is the repeated, two-part accompaniment to the Verse. This simple, clean tone guitar pattern is varied slightly between parts and as it is repeated. For the C chord in the second measure (both parts), use your ring finger on the A string (3rd fret) and middle finger on the D string (2nd fret) before finishing the phrase with your middle finger on the A string (2nd fret).

TRACK 57
Full Band

Chorus

Another two-part excerpt, this dramatic Chorus features a simple, repeated chord progression with small variations in rhythm and phrasing. For the chords that require the use of your thumb, simply hook it around the top of the fingerboard to fret the F root on the 1st fret of the low E string. For the many G chords without a third (B), position your hand as if you were playing a regular, root-position G major chord and place your index finger on the 2nd fret of the A string to muffle it.

TRACK 58
Full Band

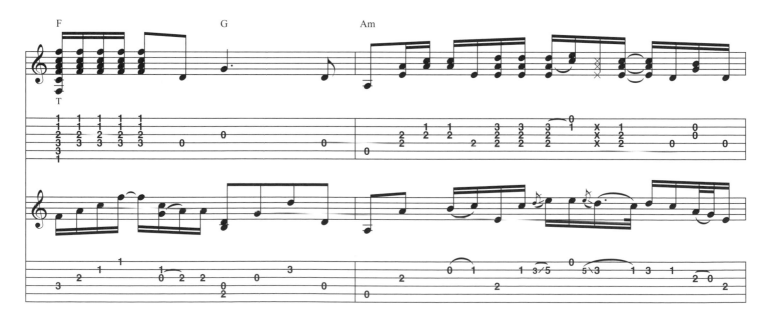

Solo

This smoldering Solo is packed with wailing bends and blues-inflected licks. Begin the Solo with your ring finger bending the G string, using your pinky to catch the Gs on the B string (8th fret) in the first two measures. For the sliding octaves in measure 3, use your index finger (flattened slightly to muffle the D string) and ring finger for the lower and higher notes, respectively. There's a classic lick in measure 5, where the B string is bent up a whole step at the 15th fret (use your ring finger, later pulled off to the index finger) and held while striking a G on the high E string at the same fret (use your pinky). To create the feedback effects at the Solo's end, you'll most likely need to crank up the amp (sorry, neighbors!). The whole thing will probably require a good deal of experimentation to recreate accurately, especially if you're not used to working with controlled feedback. You can be sure that Slash recorded this part with a massive tube amplifier cranked up in its own isolation booth. When working this out at home, try standing at different angles and distances from the amp's speaker to gauge the sensitivity of your particular setup—it's going to vary greatly from guitar to guitar, amp to amp, etc.

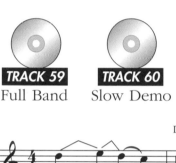

TRACK 59 — Full Band

TRACK 60 — Slow Demo

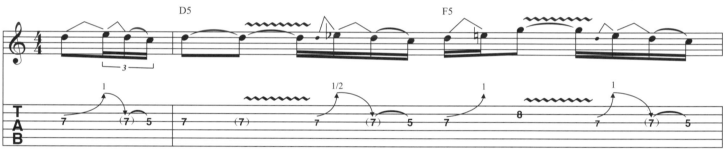

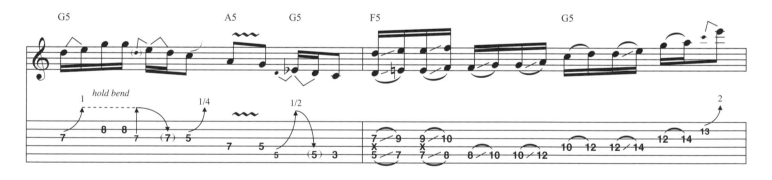

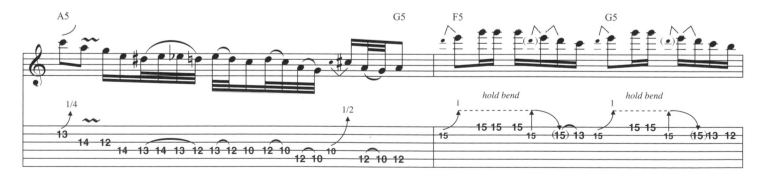

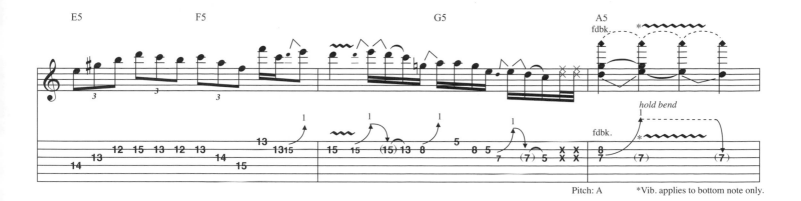

Pitch: A *Vib. applies to bottom note only.

November Rain

from *Use Your Illusion I*

Words and Music by
W. Axl Rose

"November Rain" may be best remembered for its lengthy conceptual video, which won MTV's Best Cinematography award and was the most requested video of 1992. The long (nearly nine minutes), heavily piano-driven opus reveals Axl Rose's unlikely Elton John influence, but still features some intense and emotional solo work by Slash, which is our focus here.

First Solo

This soulful Solo makes good use of simple melodic devices. This is a more mature Slash than we've heard on earlier recordings, though it should be said that he's always shown rare taste and restraint for a hard rock guitarist. The Solo begins with a B string bend using the ring finger at the 8th fret; fret the Cs that follow on the high E string with your pinky. The final bend in measure 2 should be taken by your index finger. Notice how Slash returns to his opening idea in measures 5 and 6 before spinning off into a variation. The bent C at the end of measure 6 should be played with your pinky before shifting your hand to allow your ring finger to bend the D at the start of measure 7. Begin measure 11 by bending the high E string (12th fret) up a half step with your index finger before jumping up to the C at the 20th fret with your ring finger. The descending phrase that begins at the end of that measure should be fretted by your middle finger alone, sliding down the neck, until the last four notes of measure 12. The final phrases in measures 15 and 16 should be played with your index finger taking the Fs at the 10th fret of the G string; hammer and pull with your ring finger, then slide the index down to the 9th fret before nailing the high C with your pinky. The third time through the phrase, hit the D on the B string (15th fret) with your ring finger, bend it up a whole step, and then hold it while your pinky grabs the G on the high E string.

TRACK 61
Full Band

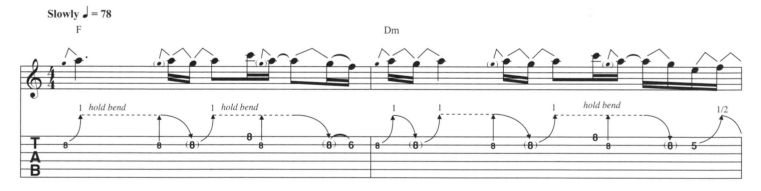

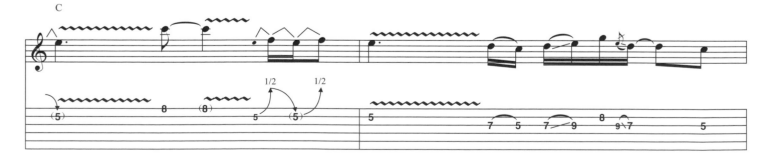

Second Solo

This second Solo continues many of the ideas begun in the previous one, helping to lend a sense of unity to the song as a whole. Begin by tracing the D Dorian mode (D, E, F, G, A, B, C) up the G string before landing on the F (18th fret of the B string) with your index finger. The familiar bends that follow should be executed by your middle finger (20th fret of the B string), with your ring finger grabbing the notes on the high E string. The bent B in measure 5 of the example, pushed up a half step to the chord's root, can be played with either your middle or ring fingers. The bends on the 17th fret of the B string in the measures that follow should be executed with your index finger, allowing you to stay in position for the twisty, scalar line that ends the Solo.

TRACK 62
Full Band

Outro Solo

"November Rain" takes a left turn around the seven-minute mark, unfolding into a lengthy "epilogue" section in C minor. The example below is part of Slash's Solo that runs until the song's end and pivots continually between the opening, three-measure motif built on the C harmonic minor scale (C, D, E♭, F, G, A♭, B) and furious metal licks that answer in the two measures that follow. Begin with your ring finger at the 20th fret of the high E string, allowing you to execute the bend with the support of your other fingers. The line in measures 4 and 5 is long and difficult, so take the time to work it up to speed. Begin with your middle finger on the A♭ on the 16th fret of the high E string and stay in position (using your index finger for the B string bends in measure 5) on what is essentially a lengthy trip up and down the scale. After repeating the three-measure motif in measures 6–8, the example ends with another extremely challenging line, this time culled from the C natural minor scale (C, D, E♭, F, G, A♭, B♭); the natural minor scale is often referred to as the Aeolian mode. As with the previous line, stay in 15th position, with your index finger fretting all notes on the 15th fret, your middle finger the notes on the 16th fret, and so on. You'll need to shift down at the end of the line to hammer on and pull off between B♭ and A♭ on the G string (13th and 15th frets), before ending on that vibrato-laden D.

TRACK 63
Full Band

TRACK 64
Slow Demo

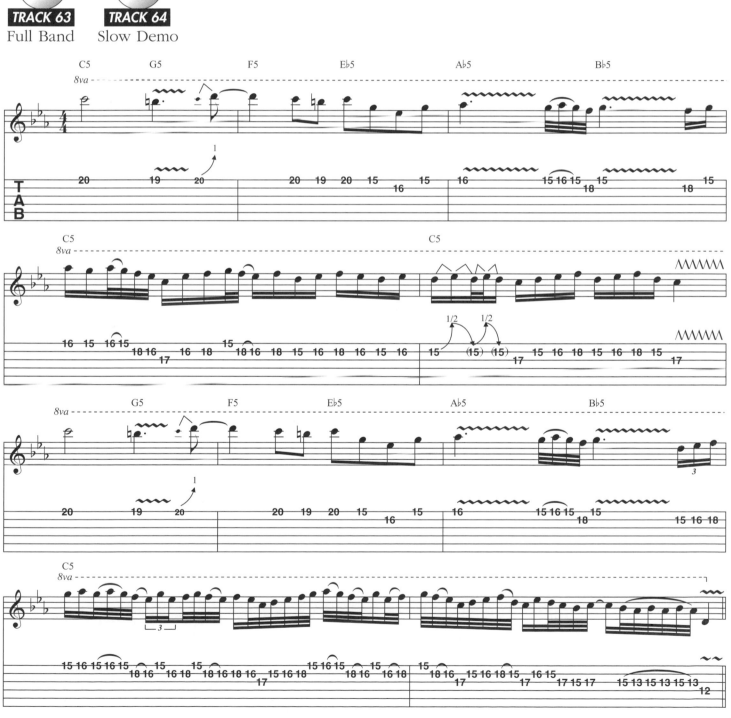

67

Knockin' on Heaven's Door

from *Use Your Illusion II*

Words and Music by
by Bob Dylan

Bob Dylan's folk classic, already remade by Bob Marley and Eric Clapton, got another facelift in the hands of Guns N' Roses. Appearing on the soundtrack of the Tom Cruise film *Days of Thunder*, "Knockin'" was one of the many reasons the *Use Your Illusion* records shot to the top of the Billboard charts. The chords and rhythm guitar parts are fairly straightforward throughout, so our focus here will be on Slash's tasty soloing.

Verse

This simple progression runs the length of the tune with slight variations in the Chorus, where a C major chord replaces the earlier change to A minor. Let the chords ring out for their full durations while picking the individual notes. There are a few hammer-ons and small fingering adjustments here and there, but this is essentially a basic, folksy part that should present little challenge.

TRACK 65
Full Band

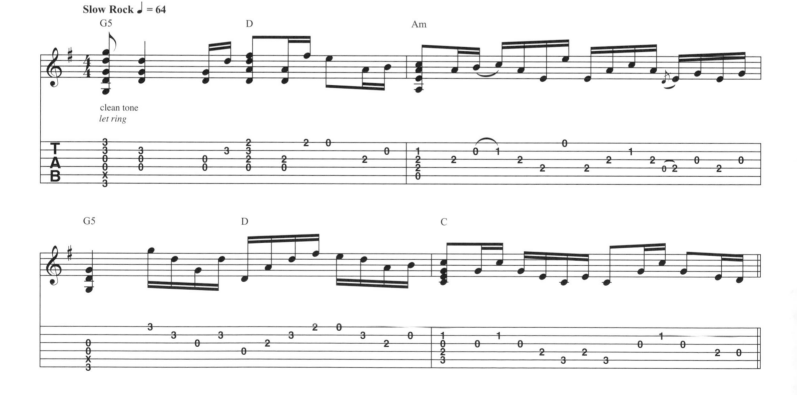

First Solo

This beautiful and thoughtful solo is a textbook example of rock guitar ballad work. Slash begins with a nod to Eric Clapton, paraphrasing a classic line by the master. Begin with your ring finger executing the bends on the G string (14th fret), allowing your pinky to grab the D on the B string (15th fret). In measure 3, use your ring finger to slide up the B string from the 15th to the 17th fret, leaving your middle finger to execute the bent C at the 13th fret. Once again, use your ring finger to play the bends in measures 5–8. Strive for pitch accuracy and a clean, warmly distorted sound. Slash's classic tones and eternal deference to the song at hand—rather than "guitar hero" flashiness—are ample evidence of a truly superior musician.

TRACK 66
Full Band

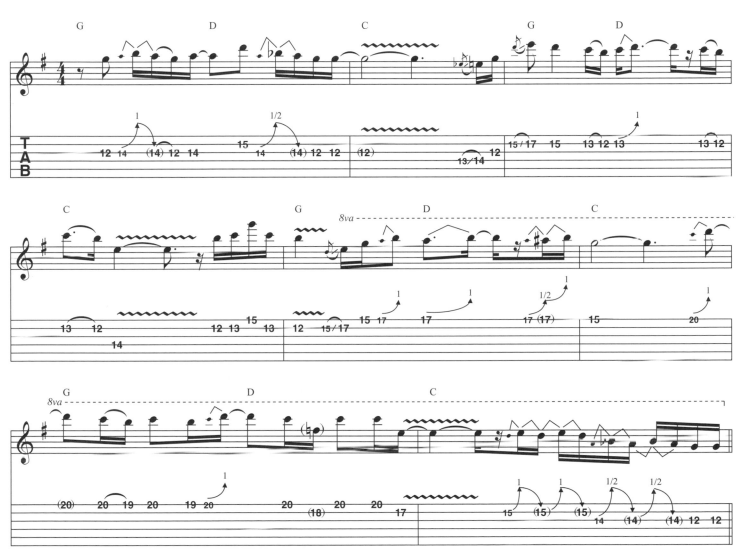

Second Solo

More melodic and emotional playing makes "Knockin'" a real treat for guitarists, especially those looking to add to their own vocabulary by copping a few choice licks here and there. Don't be apprehensive about taking your favorite Slash licks and adding them to your arsenal—it's hard to play any style convincingly without knowing the "language," so to speak, and the study of great players only helps to build your own chops. I'm not saying that you should learn every Slash solo note-for-note and play it back verbatim; rather, every once in a while concentrate on an individual lick and examine how it can be incorporated into your own playing. Then, grab some more from your other favorite players. Mix and match, and try to view each new piece of musical data as a building block towards your own unique style. We should each try to find our original and individual voice on our instrument, but it's nearly impossible to exist in a vacuum or without influences.

That said, let's take a look at the Solo itself. Begin with your middle finger at the 13th fret of the B string. You can use either your middle or ring finger to execute the first bend, but you'll definitely want to use your ring finger in measure 2 to bend the B string. In measure 3, use your middle finger to bend the G string up and hold it while your ring finger barres the B and high E strings at the 15th fret. The high E string bends in measure 4 should be taken by your middle finger, allowing you to shift up for the following measure where your ring finger will need to execute the stratospheric bends at the 20th and 22nd frets. You'll need to use your middle finger in measure 6 to bend the B string at the 22nd fret while your ring finger catches the D on the high E string. From there, the Solo winds down with descending phrases ending in a sustained G on the low E string that decays with controlled, musical feedback. Notice once again how skillfully Slash takes us back to the vocal, with ideas that help to shape the song both musically and emotionally.

TRACK 67
Full Band

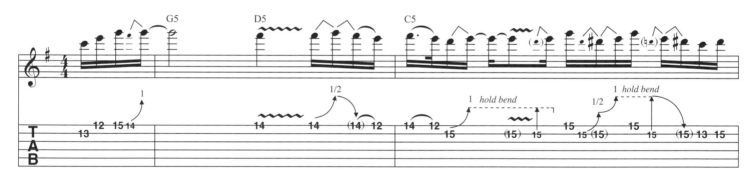

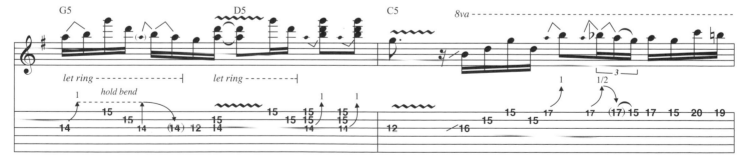

*Refers to fdbk. only.

Pretty Tied Up
(The Perils of Rock N' Roll Decadence)

from **Use Your Illusion II**

Words and Music by
W. Axl Rose, Slash,
Duff McKagan and Izzy Stradlin

After all of the ballads, epic production pieces, and covers, it's fitting that we end up here, with a straight-ahead rock tune decrying the excesses of fast-living superstardom. Penned by Izzy, "Pretty Tied Up" manages to incorporate electric sitar into its Intro but nevertheless returns us to Guns N' Roses' roots—1980s-style metal with gritty, honest lyrics that poke fun at a band that never took itself too seriously to begin with. Who else could find a way to include the lyric "cool ranch dressing" anyway?

Chorus

This rollicking Chorus is split between Izzy's chunky power chords (the chord symbols above the staff) and Slash's looser, upper register playing and scratchy muted strings. Play all of the double stops at the 12th fret with your ring finger barring and bending the G and B strings. Be sure to use an even pick attack throughout and play only the open A and D strings in measures 10 and 11 of the example (try to make them equal in volume to the chords that precede them). Play the final, single-note phrase with your ring finger barring the 7th fret and your index finger fretting the last note on the G string.

TRACK 68
Full Band

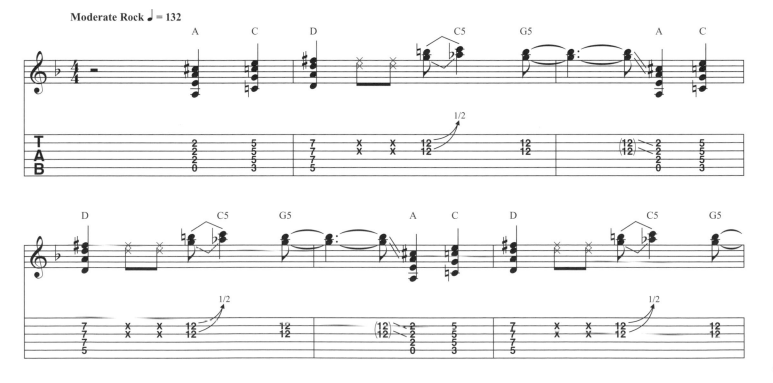

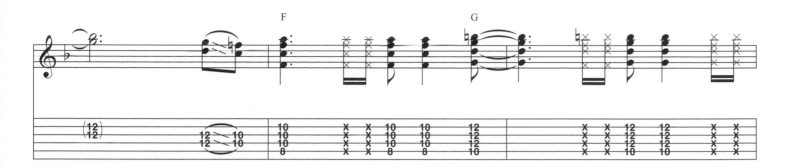

First Solo

Slash captures the essence of "Pretty Tied Up" with this traditional, wailing heavy metal Solo, built mainly from the D Dorian mode (D, E, F, G, A, B, C). The example begins with a repeated bending phrase on the B and high E strings. Use your ring finger to do the bending, rolling it from the high E to the B string at the 13th fret in measure 4. Play the double stop phrase in measure 6 with barres by your index finger at the 10th fret and ring finger at the 12th fret. As usual, the ring finger executes the remainder of the bends, save for an index finger bend in measure 11 where the F on the 13th fret of the high E string is pushed up a half step. Begin the 16th notes in measure 15 with your pinky at the 13th fret, allowing you to stay in 10th position (index finger anchored at the 10th fret) until the Solo's completion.

TRACK 69
Full Band

TRACK 70
Slow Demo

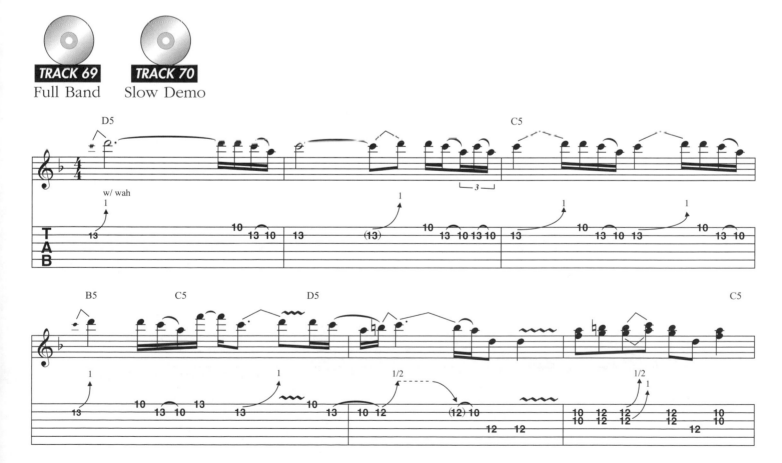

Outro Solo

Here are more fiery licks and lines as the Chorus repeats and heads for the fade-out. This time, our excerpt is constructed mainly of notes from the D blues scale (D, F, G, G#, A, C), with a few exceptions here and there (mostly Bs and Es—notes borrowed from the Dorian mode). There shouldn't be anything too surprising here if you've worked your way through this book; once again, let patience and diligence be your guides as you put this Solo together. Be sure to check out the lick that stretches from measures 10 through 14; it's a classic phrase that Slash puts through some tricky rhythmic permutations.

TRACK 71
Full Band

TRACK 72
Slow Demo

Pretty Tied Up *Cont.*

It's often been said that hard work is its own reward, and that axiom applies here as well as anywhere. Behind the sunglasses, massive hair, and drunken, swaggering demeanor, Slash is a musician of rare taste and skill, one who has honed his craft through long hours of practice and performance. Whether you've bought this book to expand and improve your playing, or because you're a ravenous Guns N' Roses fan, your own reward will be equal to the amount of work you put into your playing. In the end, you'll be a stronger, more confident guitarist for it. We're all the sum product of our influences, in addition to whatever unique perspectives we bring to the music, and in this way the tradition is carried forth. When you allow a little Slash to creep into your playing, you're also inviting in all the great players who influenced him—Jimmy Page, Jeff Beck, Jimi Hendrix, Billy Gibbons, Keith Richards, Tony Iommi, Pete Townshend, and all the rest. Good luck.

GUITAR NOTATION LEGEND

Guitar music can be notated three different ways: on a *musical staff*, in *tablature*, and in *rhythm slashes*.

RHYTHM SLASHES are written above the staff. Strum chords in the rhythm indicated. Use the chord diagrams found at the top of the first page of the transcription for the appropriate chord voicings. Round noteheads indicate single notes.

THE MUSICAL STAFF shows pitches and rhythms and is divided by bar lines into measures. Pitches are named after the first seven letters of the alphabet.

TABLATURE graphically represents the guitar fingerboard. Each horizontal line represents a string, and each number represents a fret.

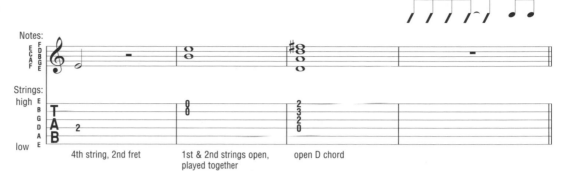

4th string, 2nd fret

1st & 2nd strings open, played together

open D chord

HALF-STEP BEND: Strike the note and bend up 1/2 step.

WHOLE-STEP BEND: Strike the note and bend up one step.

GRACE NOTE BEND: Strike the note and immediately bend up as indicated.

SLIGHT (MICROTONE) BEND: Strike the note and bend up 1/4 step.

BEND AND RELEASE: Strike the note and bend up as indicated, then release back to the original note. Only the first note is struck.

PRE-BEND: Bend the note as indicated, then strike it.

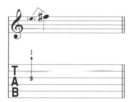

VIBRATO: The string is vibrated by rapidly bending and releasing the note with the fretting hand.

WIDE VIBRATO: The pitch is varied to a greater degree by vibrating with the fretting hand.

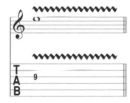

HAMMER-ON: Strike the first (lower) note with one finger, then sound the higher note (on the same string) with another finger by fretting it without picking.

PULL-OFF: Place both fingers on the notes to be sounded. Strike the first note and without picking, pull the finger off to sound the second (lower) note.

LEGATO SLIDE: Strike the first note and then slide the same fret-hand finger up or down to the second note. The second note is not struck.

SHIFT SLIDE: Same as legato slide, except the second note is struck.

TRILL: Very rapidly alternate between the notes indicated by continuously hammering on and pulling off.

TAPPING: Hammer ("tap") the fret indicated with the pick-hand index or middle finger and pull off to the note fretted by the fret hand.

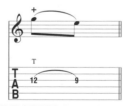

NATURAL HARMONIC: Strike the note while the fret-hand lightly touches the string directly over the fret indicated.

PINCH HARMONIC: The note is fretted normally and a harmonic is produced by adding the edge of the thumb or the tip of the index finger of the pick hand to the normal pick attack.

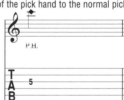

PICK SCRAPE: The edge of the pick is rubbed down (or up) the string, producing a scratchy sound.

MUFFLED STRINGS: A percussive sound is produced by laying the fret hand across the string(s) without depressing, and striking them with the pick hand.

PALM MUTING: The note is partially muted by the pick hand lightly touching the string(s) just before the bridge.

RAKE: Drag the pick across the strings indicated with a single motion.

TREMOLO PICKING: The note is picked as rapidly and continuously as possible.

VIBRATO BAR DIVE AND RETURN: The pitch of the note or chord is dropped a specified number of steps (in rhythm), then returned to the original pitch.

VIBRATO BAR SCOOP: Depress the bar just before striking the note, then quickly release the bar.

VIBRATO BAR DIP: Strike the note and then immediately drop a specified number of steps, then release back to the original pitch.

Great DVD selections from CHERRY LANE

Steven Adler's Getting Started with Rock Drumming
taught by the Legendary Former Guns N' Roses Drummer!
02501387 DVD $29.99

Altered Tunings and Techniques for Modern Metal Guitar
taught by Rick Plunkett
02501457 DVD $19.99

Beginning Blues Guitar
RHYTHM AND SOLOS
taught by Al Ek
02501325 DVD $19.99

Black Label Society
featuring Danny Gill
Guitar Legendary Licks
02500983 2-DVD Set $29.95

Black Sabbath
featuring Danny Gill
Guitar Legendary Licks
02500874 DVD $24.95

Blues Masters by the Bar
taught by Dave Celentano
02501146 DVD $24.99

Children of Bodom
ALEXI LAIHO'S LEGENDARY LICKS
taught by Danny Gill
02501398 DVD $24.99

John Denver
featuring Nate LaPointe
Guitar Legendary Licks
02500917 DVD $24.95

Learn to Play the Songs of Bob Dylan
taught by Nate LaPointe
Guitar Legendary Licks
02500918 DVD $24.95

Funky Rhythm Guitar
taught by Buzz Feiten
02501393 DVD $24.99

Grateful Dead – Classic Songs
featuring Nate LaPointe
Guitar Legendary Licks
02500968 DVD $24.95

Grateful Dead
featuring Nate LaPointe
Guitar Legendary Licks
02500551 DVD $24.95

Guitar Heroes
taught by Danny Gill
Guitar Legendary Licks
02501069 2-DVD Set $29.95

The Latin Funk Connection
02501417 DVD $19.99

Metallica – 1983-1988
featuring Doug Boduch
Bass Legendary Licks
02500481 DVD $24.95

Metallica – 1988-1997
featuring Doug Boduch
Bass Legendary Licks
02500484 DVD $24.95

Metallica – 1983-1988
featuring Nathan Kilen
Drum Legendary Licks
02500482 DVD $24.95

Metallica – 1988-1997
featuring Nathan Kilen
Drum Legendary Licks
02500485 DVD $24.95

Metallica – 1983-1988
featuring Doug Boduch
Guitar Legendary Licks
02500479 DVD $24.95

Metallica – 1988-1997
featuring Doug Boduch
Guitar Legendary Licks
02500480 DVD $24.99

Mastering the Modes for the Rock Guitarist
taught by Dave Celentano
02501449 DVD $19.99

Home Recording Magazine's 100 Recording Tips and Tricks
STRATEGIES AND SOLUTIONS FOR YOUR HOME STUDIO
02500509 DVD $19.95

Ozzy Osbourne – The Randy Rhoads Years
featuring Danny Gill
Guitar Legendary Licks
02501301 2-DVD Set $29.99

Pink Floyd – Learn the Songs from Dark Side of the Moon
by Nate LaPointe
Guitar Legendary Licks
02500919 DVD $24.95

See your local music retailer or contact

Rock Harmonica
taught by Al Ek
02501475 DVD $19.99

Poncho Sanchez
featuring the Poncho Sanchez Latin Jazz Band
02500729 DVD $24.95

Joe Satriani
featuring Danny Gill
Guitar Legendary Licks Series
02500767 2-DVD Set $29.95

Joe Satriani – Classic Songs
featuring Danny Gill
Guitar Legendary Licks
02500913 2-DVD Set $29.95

Johnny Winter
taught by Al Ek
Guitar Legendary Licks
02501307 2-DVD Set 29.99

Johnny Winter
SLIDE GUITAR
featuring Johnny Winter with instruction by Al Ek
Guitar Legendary Licks
02501042 DVD $29.95

Wolfmother
featuring Danny Gill
02501062 DVD $24.95

cherry lane
music company

EXCLUSIVELY DISTRIBUTED BY
HAL•LEONARD CORPORATION
7777 W. BLUEMOUND RD. P.O. BOX 13819 MILWAUKEE, WI 53213
Prices, contents, and availability subject to change without notice.

061

 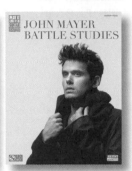